TESCO
Every little helps

£1.50

Gi

...emic Index
...ested

the
Gi GUIDE

Understanding the Glycaemic Index,
healthy eating, lifestyle and shopping

Rick Gallop
& Hamish Renton

Virgin BOOKS

Useful links
www.raceforlife.org
www.runnersworld.co.uk
www.britishcycling.org.uk
www.dh.gov.uk
www.tescodiets.com
www.i-village.co.uk
www.tesco.com/healthyliving

This edition published in Great Britain in 2005 by
Virgin Books
Thames Wharf Studios
Rainville Road
London W6 9HA

Reprinted in 2005

ISBN 0 7535 1033 2
Designed by Smith & Gilmour, London
Printed and bound in the UK by Bath Press, CPI Group

Contents

Foreword by Sir Steve Redgrave CBE

Although I have spent years of hard training and have learned how to eat a sensible and nutritious diet, I have been really encouraged to find out more about the Glycaemic Index and am very impressed by the work undertaken by Tesco in this area of food information.

I am therefore very supportive of Hamish, Rick and Tesco in their efforts to bring Gi into the mainstream in a way that is simple and makes sense. Having had the chance to read this book I am delighted that the authors have presented Gi in such an accessible way and feel sure that by following the principles in these pages you can improve your health and your waistline.

Although a seasoned Olympian and endurance athlete, I had to rethink significantly how and what I was eating when I developed diabetes some years ago. Adopting the Gi plan is positive and beneficial not only to those who control their diet for healthier living but also it may help anyone at risk of developing the disease. I respect the condition but it does not rule my life and initiatives like the Gi plan make this so much easier. This book shows that Gi is for everyone, not just those who are at risk of diabetes and other life-changing disorders such as heart disease, or those in need of shedding some weight, but for all of us who would like to be healthy and stay healthy.

A message from Michel Montignac

As an obese child, teenager and young adult, I tried desperately to lose weight. Like millions of other overweight people, I never succeeded – eating less just didn't work.

Those low-calorie/low-fat diets proved to be total failures and, worse still, the resulting yo-yo effect on my weight was positively unhealthy.

At the end of the 1970s, when I was working in the pharmaceutical industry, I read about the Glycaemic Index (Gi). It was a scientific article that everyone seemed to ignore at the time. It reported on an experiment which showed that choosing carbohydrates according to their Gi value might stabilise or even reduce the risk of Type II diabetes. I noticed that more than 85% of people with diabetes were obese, so I wondered – could I use Gi to lose weight?

I followed my experimental Gi programme for three months and lost more than 30 pounds. This was fantastic! The seemingly simple Gi concept started me on the long road to developing the principles of an original and revolutionary dieting method. It became my life's work and, twenty years later, despite opposition from some academics, the Montignac Method is no longer just a theory – it has become a scientifically accepted concept. My work and that of others has completed our understanding of how the metabolic chain leads to either fat storage or to fat burning, depending on the Gi of the food in question.

Over the years I have tried, in a small way, to turn the Gi concept into a food-shopping experience. I therefore admire and applaud Tesco's decision to label a range of products with a Gi rating. This will help millions of shoppers to make healthier food choices so that the Gi will soon become the most important factor for health-conscious people.

Introduction

If you have picked up this book, you've either done so out of general curiosity or maybe because you recognise the term 'GI' and have wondered what it is all about. Well, the concept of the GI, or Glycaemic Index to give it its full name, is not new, but research has proved over recent years that it is a beneficial way of assessing your food intake.

The authors of this book have both experienced those benefits. In Rick Gallop's case, it led to his writing the bestselling *The Gi Diet* and *Living the Gi Diet*. His co-author, Hamish Renton, who works for Tesco, was so impressed by the weight loss that he achieved with *The Gi Diet*, that he was convinced that Tesco should be helping its customers by labelling as many of their products as possible to show whether they had a 'low' or 'medium' GI rating.

Here's Hamish's story:

In 2003, my wife Kate and I had a beautiful baby boy, a brother for a very active two-year-old daughter. This was a time of great happiness, but also an incredibly tiring experience! Like any working parent with young children, I found that I was often very tired in the afternoons. I began to notice that the major factor affecting my energy levels in the afternoon was what I had eaten for lunch. I felt most lethargic when I ate certain foods, usually ones that didn't seem to be unhealthy such as baked potatoes, rice or French sticks. I normally ate at 12.30 pm and by 1.30 pm I would be really sleepy. By 3.00 pm I would be hungry again – not great as my desk was very close to the chocolate-tasting team! So, I found myself in a vicious circle of eating to keep up my energy levels, but ending up more tired.

I read about the GI being linked with good energy levels and discovered that lower GI foods were digested more slowly, keeping energy levels constant, and so were more filling than higher GI foods.

I decided to give it a go and followed a few of the suggestions; for example, eating porridge oats for breakfast and swapping white bread for granary. I was amazed at the difference. I didn't have any mid-afternoon tiredness slumps.

I discovered that foods were ranked in a league table called the Glycaemic Index, but I found looking up the GI ratings for my favourite foods difficult, as there was virtually no information on UK products. I knew that many in Tesco, including a colleague, Tim Mason, had had very positive experiences in the 1990s using the Montignac Method – devised by the father of GI, Michel Montignac. This inspired me to explore GI further. I was so convinced by the theory behind GI eating that I set about finding out which of my favourite Tesco products were lower GI foods. These formed the basis of my meals. Once I had started eating the GI way, I found that I had more energy, and was losing weight effortlessly. This enabled me to begin a programme of walking/jogging that, in time, has become a comprehensive running programme concluding in the London marathon, with the Tesco Triathlon a goal for 2005.

By coincidence, Rick Gallop's *The Gi Diet* had been published in 2003 and was also proving a big hit with readers who followed its advice. As Rick followed his first book with a second in spring 2004, so Hamish was convincing Tesco that they should be investing in the testing of 250 of Tesco's most popular products in the laboratories at Oxford's Brookes, Reading and Melbourne Universities to find out which ones were low and medium GI. The results are included at the back of the book and cover a whole host of different foods.

Hamish asked Rick to come on board to provide his experience of diet and nutrition and show how the GI can be used to eat healthily and, for many, to lose weight. In this book you will discover what the Glycaemic Index is all about and how you can put it into practice.

1 What is the Glycaemic Index?

The Glycaemic Index (GI) is a medical term for measuring the speed at which various foods in our digestive system break down into glucose – and this is the body's source of energy. By indexing glucose at 100, all other foods are calculated against that index. So for example, the cereal cornflakes, which digests quickly, has a Glycaemic Index of 77, but porridge is calculated at 42 as it digests more slowly, and yoghurt is even lower at 14. The foods that are measured by the Gi contain carbohydrates (carbs) and these are our principal source of energy.

To answer how knowing about Gi helps you to make healthy food choices, we should take a step back and look at how carbohydrates fit into overall nutrition.

All foods fall into the following four main food groups: bread, other cereals and potatoes; fruit and vegetables; milk and dairy foods and meat, fish and alternatives. There is a fifth group of foods that contain fat and foods containing sugar and these should make up the smallest part of one's diet and most people need to eat less of them. These groups contain varying proportions of all or some of the main nutrients which are protein, carbohydrates and fats. So let's examine each of these three food groups and shed some light on to the subject.

THE LOWDOWN ON FOODS

Proteins

Proteins are an essential part of your diet. One half of your body weight is made up of protein, including muscles, organs, skin and hair. Protein is required to build and repair body tissue. Proteins also slow down the digestive process, which, as we will see shortly, is key to controlling blood sugar levels and keeping you feeling alert, full and satisfied.

As protein is found in a broad range of foods, both animal and vegetable, it is important to choose the right sort. Red meat and dairy foods, for example, are good sources of protein, but they can also be loaded with saturated fats, which we will talk more about in the next section. So the best sources for protein are those that are:

- low-fat meats trimmed of any visible fat
- skinless poultry
- seafood (not battered or breaded)
- low-fat dairy foods
- eggs
- soya-based products (e.g. Tesco Soya Milk), and even
- the humble bean (e.g. kidney beans).

Protein should be consumed at all your meals throughout the day. We tend to be protein-light at breakfast and lunch and it is not until dinner when most of us consume our main protein quotient. Protein is also a critical brain food providing essential neurotransmitters (chemical messengers) that relay messages to the brain, so you need a constant supply throughout the day to keep you alert with an active mind.

Fats

Fats are possibly the most misunderstood of the three food categories and traditionally the villain in weight control. Let's get the facts straight. Fats are absolutely essential to your diet and your digestive process. Fat does not necessarily make you fat – the amount you eat does. That's something that's difficult to control as fat tastes, well, terrific! Your body loves it because it doesn't have to waste a lot of energy in converting fat into those fat cells around your waist and hips. Your body will do everything to encourage you to eat more.

Fat contains more than twice the calories of protein or carbohydrates, so the quantity we eat is critical.

It's not just how much fat we eat, it's also what type of fat we eat that can have a serious impact on our health, particularly heart problems, stroke, some major cancers, such as prostate and colon, and even Alzheimer's.

Rick's view is that there are four types of fat: awful, bad, good and best. The ones to avoid are called 'hydrogenated' or 'trans' fats and these consist of vegetable oils that have been heat-treated to make them thicken at room temperature. They are frequently found in cakes, biscuits and snacks.

The other 'bad' fats are 'saturated' fats and are easily recognisable as they come from animal sources and are always solid at room temperatures, for example butter, cheese and fatty meats.

The 'good' fats are exclusively vegetable-based oils such as corn and sunflower oils, which are called 'polyunsaturated' and 'monounsaturated'. Your best choice amongst these oils are those that are highest in monounsaturated fats such as olive and rapeseed oils. These oils have a beneficial effect on cholesterol levels and are good for your heart. Olive oil is used extensively in the Mediterranean countries where they have low rates of heart disease. The two exceptions are coconut and palm oil (often called tropical oils), which may sound healthy but are in fact the only vegetable oils that are saturated fats. Because they are cheap they are found frequently in snack foods, packaged biscuits and baked goods. Try and avoid them.

While on the subject of health, especially heart health, some oils contain a wonderful substance called 'omega-3', which is found in deep-sea fish, such as salmon, as well as in flaxseed and rapeseed oils. The Nutricentre (see page 140) offers a range of omega-3 supplements.

So the two things you should remember about fats are the *quantity* and the *type of fat*. Although many of us have tried to lower our fat intake by eating leaner cuts of meat and reduced-fat milk, we have also been eating more cheese and ice cream. Also many of today's popular foods such as snacks, cereals and fast foods contain hidden fats. As a result, the total fat consumption in our diets, contrary to popular belief, has not changed significantly.

What has changed significantly is our consumption of carbohydrates, the third of our three food categories.

Carbohydrates

Carbohydrates are the main source of energy for your body and should account for 50% of your calorie intake. (Proteins typically account for 15% and fat 35% of your daily Calories [kcals].) They are also essential for your health.

Carbohydrates are found mainly in grains, vegetables, fruits, legumes (beans and pulses) and dairy products. Your digestive system converts carbohydrates to glucose, which dissolves into your bloodstream and is transported to those parts of your body that use energy, such as your muscles and brain. Surprisingly, the brain can use up to two-thirds of the glucose in your system.

While they do contain starch and sugar, many carbohydrates are also rich in fibre, vitamins, minerals and antioxidants, all of which play a critical role in your health and help protect you from major diseases such as heart disease, stroke and cancer. This is why many nutritional and medical authorities are questioning the effects on health of some of today's popular low-carb, high-fat diets. By minimising carbohydrates you run the risk of depriving your body of many essential nutrients as indicated above. There is little gain in improving your health by losing weight while at the same time putting your health at risk with a diet that is short-changing your nutritional needs.

As with fats, it's not just how much carbohydrate we consume, it's what type of carbohydrate that is equally important. A little history is necessary here and it is a fascinating story.

HISTORY OF FOOD PROCESSING

Concurrent with the retreating glaciers of the ice age 10,000 years ago, grains (or cereals) started being cultivated for the first time. Egypt was the bread basket of the ancient world and much of their wealth came from grain production. Grain grew to become the staple food in the western world much as rice has in the eastern regions. Grains were ground by giant grinding stones propelled by air or water.

Then came the food revolution: only a couple of generations or so ago, modern high-speed steel rolling mills ground up the grain, at the same time stripping away all the fibre, oils and nutrients to form a fine white flour. This fine white flour is a basic ingredient in most of our breads, cereals, cakes and snack foods such as crackers, tortillas/corn chips, pretzels and biscuits. Our grain consumption has increased by up to 50% over the last three decades.

The same revolution in food processing has had an impact on other key carbohydrates such as fruits and vegetables. About 100 years ago, most people ate food that came straight from the farm to the dinner table. With new technology all that changed. Along came prepared and processed foods. Convenience was the buzzword. Again, this has had huge effects on the nutritional and health value of the original foods. All the great food companies such as Kraft, Nestlé and Kellogg only started processing and packaging natural foods in the past century.

We now know that proteins, fats and carbohydrates make up our diets. We also know that, for nutrition and good health, it is not just the quantity of these foods we eat that matters, it's also the quality. So with this in mind, let's now look to the role that the Glycaemic Index (Gi) plays in all this.

HOW DOES GI WORK FOR ME?

As we discussed at the outset, the Gi measures the speed at which food breaks down in our digestive system into glucose, the body's source of energy. Here are some examples of Gi ratings:

EXAMPLE OF GI RATINGS

HIGH GI FOODS	RATING	LOW GI FOODS	RATING
Sugar	100	Orange	44
Baguette	95	All Bran	43
Cornflakes	84	Oatmeal	42
Rice cakes	82	Spaghetti	41
Doughnut	76	Apple	38
Bagel	72	Beans	31
Cereal bar	72	Grapefruit	25
Biscuits (plain)	69	Yogurt	14

Any food rating less than 55 in the Gi is considered low

The Gi rating of a food is important to nutrition and health because:
• low Gi foods tend to have more nutritional (or healthy) content than the high Gi foods, which are usually highly processed. This is important for your health.
• low Gi foods break down in your digestive system more slowly, leaving you feeling more satiated for a longer period of time so you don't go hungry. This is critical for weight control.
• low Gi foods are important for managing diseases, such as diabetes where controlling blood sugar levels is essential.
Let's deal with each of these in turn:

Nutrition

You can easily see in the table on the previous page many highly processed foods tend to be high Gi, meaning that most of the original fibre and nutrients have been stripped away. Conversely most of the low Gi foods on the right are more in their natural state with their nutritional benefits intact.

If there is one thing that nutritionists and the medical profession agree upon, it is that diets rich in fruits, vegetables, whole grains, legumes and low-fat dairy foods are essential for good health and the very large majority of these foods are low Gi.

Weight control

High Gi foods such as sugary breakfast cereals digest quickly and by mid-morning you are hungry again and looking for your next sugar fix.

Conversely, take traditional breakfast porridge oats, the sort many of us haven't had since we were kids. Porridge is low Gi and digests more slowly so you are not hungry by the time you get to work. Though you need to avoid adding sugar!

Low Gi foods leave you feeling fuller for longer, and enable you to control your appetite and therefore your weight. The next chapter talks about the Gi and weight loss in more detail.

Many of Tesco's own-brand products have now been tested to find their Gi level and they can be found in the food listing beginning on page 118. They have been divided into three colour-coded categories to indicate whether they are high Gi (red), medium Gi (yellow) or low Gi (green).

Diabetes

Because low Gi foods break down more slowly, it means that the supply of glucose into the bloodstream is more gradual and therefore helps moderate blood sugar levels. Chapter 5 looks at the impact of the Glycaemic Index on health, including diabetes.

What affects the Gi of foods?

THE ROLE OF PROTEIN AND FAT

Though the Gi is based on carbohydrates, it is also profoundly influenced by protein and fat, both of which act as brakes on your digestive system. Most carbohydrate-based foods also contain both fats and proteins. For instance, some vegetables are a good source of oils, and beans a good source of protein. Also when we eat a meal we are usually combining all three food categories in our stomach.

So low Gi carbohydrates, low-fat proteins, and good fats/oils are the ideal combination of foods for a healthy and nutritious diet.

In the next chapter we will focus on one of the principal health benefits of eating the Gi way: weight loss and weight control.

FIBRE

Fibre comes in two forms:

• Soluble fibre, which is soluble in water, thickens food, thus slowing down its passage through your digestive tract.
• Insoluble fibre acts as a physical barrier to the digestive enzymes and again slows down the digestive process.

That is one reason why foods high in soluble fibre such as fruits, oats and beans are low Gi foods. Foods such as 100% bran breakfast cereals and whole grains are high in insoluble fibre and are again low Gi.

IMPACT OF COOKING AND PROCESSING

Any processing of food will raise the Gi, because processing, usually cooking, is the first step in breaking down food into glucose. This is, in effect, digestion taking place outside your body. For instance, if you have ever had the misfortune to eat a raw potato, you will know that it is almost indigestible and tummy ache is virtually guaranteed. On the other hand, if you eat a baked potato, which is high Gi, it digests extremely quickly. In this case the cooking process is the only variable and demonstrates how cooking starts breaking down the starch capsules and fibre, making it easier for your digestive juices to get to work. So when you are cooking foods, especially vegetables, slightly undercook them. This will both help to reduce the loss of vitamins and other essential nutrients as well as keep the Gi low.

One other popular food that you should undercook is pasta. Italians call this *al dente* or 'firm to the bite'. This not only tastes better, but also helps keep the Gi lower.

Tinned food products have been subjected to very high temperatures in the canning process to avoid spoilage. Tinned soups are a good example. A tin of soup can sometimes have double the Gi when compared to a homemade soup prepared from scratch. While it is sometimes more convenient to use tinned products, especially if you are under time pressure, try to keep these to a minimum and use fresh, dried or frozen products in preference.

Letting your body do the processing is another good reason for always eating the fruit rather than drinking its juice. This way you ensure you're getting all the full benefits, especially fibre, from the fruit rather than buying its highly processed juice. You will also be consuming fewer calories: a glass of orange juice for instance contains nearly two and a half times the calories of a fresh orange.

Rice and potatoes Rice and potatoes are two staples that have unusual Gi characteristics. They are two of the few foods that have different Gi ratings dependent on the type used.

With rice, you should preferably use long grain or basmati rice rather than the short grain (glutinous/sticky) variety frequently found in Chinese food. The Gi of the latter can be higher by 50% or more.

Potatoes also have a broad Gi range. Your best choice is boiled small new potatoes and at the other end are large baked potatoes and chips. Try not to mash potatoes as this also raises the Gi by breaking them down before eating. Remember; let your body do the processing.

SUMMARY

1. Low GI foods are less processed and more nutritious than high GI foods. This benefits your health and reduces your risk of most major diseases including heart disease, stroke, many cancers, and diabetes.

2. Low GI foods are more satiating and keep you feeling fuller for longer, which is critical for weight control and weight loss.

3. Low GI foods are helpful in controlling blood sugar levels, which is essential for managing diseases such as diabetes.

4. Let your body do the processing, not the manufacturer, and don't overcook.

2 Losing or controlling your weight with Gi

One of the most significant advantages of eating low Gi foods is being able to manage your weight. With six out of ten UK adults being overweight, one in five being obese and, even more worrying, a doubling of the number of overweight children in the past twenty years, we have a real epidemic of obesity on our hands: in fact, among Western countries, the UK is second only to the US by a whisker. Interestingly, the top four overweight countries are all English-speaking: USA, UK, Australia and Canada!

Here we examine some of the problems with dieting and show how a diet based on the Glycaemic Index can help. For more details on dieting by using the Gi, get hold of a copy of *The Gi Diet* by Rick Gallop.

PROBLEMS WITH DIETS

Virtually all diets will let you lose weight, so, with over 40% of people on a diet at any one time, why do we have a growing overweight population? The answer is surprisingly simple: people just can't stay on their diets, and there are three basic reasons for this:

- Diets make people feel hungry or deprived.
- Diets can be too complex and time-consuming with counting and measuring of Calories (kcals), carbs (carbohydrate portions), points, etc.
- Diets can affect people's health negatively.

That's why it is estimated that 95% of diets ultimately fail.

Eating the low Gi way successfully addresses each of these three reasons, so if weight loss or weight control is a problem for you or your family – including your children – then read on and find out how and why this will permanently change the way you will eat for the rest of your life. If you have found your previous attempts to lose weight were unsuccessful and a painful process, than you will be delighted with how painless and simple it is to eat the GI way to a slimmer, healthier you.

Of the three reasons listed above, the latter two are probably the most easily dealt with because, given the busy lives that most of us lead, a would-be dieter will tend to avoid anything complex and time-consuming. Also, if you do feel ill as a result of going on a diet, then you should, quite rightly, stop it immediately. The first reason for a diet failing is really the most common and here's why.

Going hungry or feeling deprived

Clearly this is the major stumbling block to anyone trying to stay on a diet. The reason is very simple. All diets work by reducing the number of daily Calories (kcals - see page 26) you eat to less than you normally need. For instance, if you are typical of the average woman, you will need around 1750–2000 Calories (kcals) per day to provide the energy your body needs to function. If you take in only 1500–1750 Calories (kcals) in the food you eat, then you will be 250 Calories (kcals) short. So, to stop you running out of energy and coming to a grinding halt, your body burns up some of its Calorie (kcals) reserves from where they are stored. And we all know that they are stored in those fat cells around our waist and hips! Over time, this usage of Calories (kcals) from our fat storage cells leads to a reduction in fat and thus a reduction in weight. This sounds simple enough, but unfortunately your body doesn't like to lose its fat reserves and tells the brain that it is hungry and needs more food.

WHERE FAT FITS IN

To understand the role of fat, a little background is required. Only a few thousand years ago, a blink of an eye in time from an anthropological viewpoint, we were hunters and gatherers. Agriculture had not been invented and we had to work hard to get our food by hunting it down or gathering it from wild plants. Sometimes game and plants were plentiful and everyone feasted. Sometimes they were scarce, particularly in winter, and everyone fasted. To tide people over the times of famine, our bodies developed an ability to store food as fat: this was increased when things were good and decreased when food was in short supply. So naturally, to avoid possible starvation, our bodies were reluctant to give up the precious fat energy stores without a fight and that is why our hunger pangs are so strong. We may have come a long way in our civilisation since then but our stomachs haven't. Evolution is a lengthy process!

ROLE OF SUGAR AND INSULIN
The key factor in the process of energy storage and retrieval is insulin. Insulin is a hormone secreted by our pancreas and it does two things extremely well:
- First, it regulates the amount of sugar (glucose) in our bloodstream, removing any excess and storing it as fat.
- Second, it acts as guardian of the fat gates, making our bodies give up their precious fat reserves only reluctantly.

So controlling insulin is the name of the game. If we stimulate the production of insulin by suddenly dumping a lot of sugar in the bloodstream, it will do its job very efficiently. Soon that sugar 'high', which makes most of us feel great, becomes a sugar 'low' as the insulin rapidly lowers the blood sugar levels. So then your tummy is looking for its next sugar fix – a low blood sugar level is the trigger for your appetite. At the same time insulin is resisting giving back its new reserves to curb this appetite.

So, to limit the amount of insulin, we need to eat foods that won't stimulate its production. And that's exactly what low Gi foods can do.

By concentrating on low Gi foods that do not raise insulin production, we are able to provide a steady supply of glucose (sugar) to our bloodstream and that means your tummy is not crying out for its next sugar fix.

We have all experienced that mid-afternoon slump when we feel drowsy and lethargic and need a jolt of something to wake us up. This is a classic example of what happens after you have had a high Gi lunch: a bagel or sandwich and maybe a biscuit or muffin to go with your cola. Wham! These foods and drinks dissolve quickly into your bloodstream and you get the good short-term feeling of a sugar high (called *hyperglycaemia*). Insulin kicks in, drains out that excess sugar from your bloodstream to store as fat around your waist and hips, and leaves you with a sugar low (*hypoglycaemia*). So you grab a Danish to give you an energy boost and your insulin charges in again ... and the yo-yo cycle starts all over again. Sound familiar?

Slow-release low Gi foods leave you feeling fuller for longer and not looking for your next sugar fix.

LOSING WEIGHT WITH LOW GI FOODS

A word of warning

As with all good things, there are exceptions. As we discussed earlier, fat also acts as a brake on our digestive system. Fat has twice the calories per gram as carbohydrates or proteins, so a low Gi food with a high fat content is clearly not going to help you lose weight.

Similarly, a low Gi food may also have a high sugar content. That again won't help you lose weight. So, if you are aiming to lose weight and you go to stock up on low Gi foods, watch out for products that have a high fat content such as dairy and chocolate. Choose low-fat dairy products and here is a tip for chocoholics: if you can't envisage life without chocolate, look for the high-cocoa versions (such as Tesco Finest 72% cocoa). Because of their high chocolate concentration, a couple of squares dissolved slowly will provide as much chocolate satisfaction as a whole bar of milk chocolate. Do not make this a regular part of your diet, but use it as a treat!

For products with high sugar content, look for versions where either a sweetener has been added, such as in yoghurt, or where it states 'no sugar added'.

In short, look for low Gi foods with low fat (particularly saturated) and low sugar levels. This is not to disparage foods that have a higher Gi. Simply, if you want to lose weight, stick to the low or medium Gi foods that are low in sugar and saturated fat. See Gi food lsitings, pages 118–38.

Meals and snacks

Lastly and most importantly is when and how often you should be eating your low Gi meals. As we discussed earlier, it is important to keep your tummy busy so that it's not looking for its next meal. We recommend three main meals: breakfast, lunch and dinner. Also three snacks: mid-morning, mid-afternoon and before bedtime.

BREAKFAST

This is the most important meal because most of us won't have eaten since dinner the night before. If you miss breakfast, then you could be without food for up to sixteen hours. The result is that you load up on snacks and pig out at other meals. So make sure you have a good low Gi breakfast containing low Gi carbs, low saturated fats and low-fat protein. If you haven't had porridge since you were a child, then do try it again. This is one of your best choices. Other breakfast suggestions and recipes can be found on pages 81–6.

LUNCH

Most of us eat lunch outside the home, so eating the low Gi way can be a problem, complicated by time pressures and the availability of restaurants or fast-food outlets in your workplace area. Your best option is to take your own lunch with you. We have some suggestions in Chapter 7 on eating outside the home (see page 66 as to how you can make your packed lunch a low Gi one. Should you prefer or have to eat out, there are suggestions on how to eat the low Gi way at restaurants, fast-food and takeaway outlets.

DINNER

Dinner is traditionally the main meal of the day and in general we tend to have more time for preparing and enjoying the meal, although this may be challenged by busy mums!

A typical dinner consists of three parts: meat or seafood; potato, pasta or rice; and vegetables. Together these foods provide proteins, fats and carbohydrates along with other minerals and vitamins essential to our health. Some people add a starter or more commonly, a dessert.

The Government's Balance of Good Health (National Food Guide) recommends that anyone over the age of five should divide the balance of these different food groups into thirds, that is vegetables on one-third of the plate, potato, rice or pasta on another third and meat, seafood or another source of protein on the final third. If you are aiming to lose weight, Rick recommends you visualise your plate slightly differently with one half containing at least two vegetables; one quarter potato, rice or pasta; and the other quarter, meat or seafood (for vegetarians, eggs, Quorn, tofu, and beans). Whenever possible it is good to add a side salad.

For choices of meats, seafood, vegetables, pasta and rice, see Chapter 3 on Shopping, page 33.

Although dessert can be a problem when eating out, it should be an integral part of your meal when at home since they can provide other sources of vitamins and minerals. There is a broad range of lower Gi options that taste great and are good for you. Most fruits and low-fat dairy foods are ideal choices. There are some delicious dessert recipes for you to try on pages 108–17.

SNACK SUGGESTIONS*

Nuts – almonds, hazelnuts

Fresh fruit – apple, orange, grapefruit

Vegetables – celery, carrots, sliced bell peppers

Low-fat dairy foods – cottage cheese, cheese (Healthy Living Low Fat Cheese Spread), yoghurt

Nutrition (cereal) bars

High-bran cereals – All Bran

Porridge

* Other snack recipes can be found in *Living the GI Diet*

SNACKS
Three low Gi snacks a day require a little planning and we list some suggestions below. Try and eat balanced snacs, i.e. those containing some carbs, fat and protein. This is particularly important if you are concerned about your blood sugar levels, especially if you have, or are at risk of having, type II diabetes (see page 53).

BEVERAGES
• **Water**: As water makes up 50–70% of our body, it is not surprising that your liquid intake is important. It facilitates the digestive process, helps flush out waste and toxins and is part of a healthy diet. Most nutritionists recommend eight glasses of water a day.

A good rule of thumb is to have a 250ml glass of water before each meal or snack. Having your stomach partly filled with liquid makes you feel full more quickly, thus reducing the temptation to overeat.

- **Skimmed milk**: This is an ideal low Gi food. Try to drink at least one glass a day, preferably two. If you want a quick boost to your protein input, this is an easy solution and it is a good source of calcium.
- **Coffee**: The problem with coffee is caffeine and the cravings it can create. Although caffeine isn't a health problem in itself, it does stimulate the production of insulin. As we know, insulin reduces blood sugar levels, which increases your appetite. This is not helpful when we are trying our best to keep our appetite under control. So avoid coffee if you are dieting. Don't despair; there are some delicious decaffeinated coffees available. If a jolt of Java is essential to your survival, then go for it, but make it one cup a day maximum.
- **Tea**: Tea has much less caffeine than coffee and has the added bonus of flavanoids (antioxidants), which are beneficial to heart health. Green tea is even better. So, tea in moderation is just fine.
- **Fruit drinks/juices**: These are high in sugar and are high Gi. Avoid these if you wish to lose weight. Fruit juices and squash have a lower Gi but are still calorie dense. Always eat the fruit (or vegetable) rather than drink its juice. You'll get more nutrient value, a lower Gi and fewer calories.
- **Alcohol**: Alcohol should definitely be avoided if you wish to lose weight. Because alcohol metabolises so quickly it creates a short-term high, but it actually lowers your blood sugar. And, unfortunately, the buzz from alcohol means you don't always want to stop after one drink. If you are drinking alcohol remember that the safe upper limits for men and women are four and three units per day respectively. Don't multiply this by seven and assume it to be a safe weekly intake. Aim to have one or two alcohol-free days each week. For reference, a 'unit' is equivalent to:

- 1 small glass (125ml) of 9% ABV wine (pub measures are generally larger than this – 175ml and even 250ml) and most wines nowadays are higher in alcohol, so these will contain more units per glass)
- half a pint of ordinary strength (3%) larger or bitter
- single measure of spirits or aperitifs (home measures tend to be larger!).

Reading labels

How do you determine what are the key ingredients in a product that affects both your health and your weight. Let's examine the label of a typical food product.

Nutrition

Typical Composition	This pack (450g) provides	100g (3¹/₄ oz) provide
Energy	1620kJ 387kcal	360kJ 86kcal
Protein	24.3g	5.4g
Carbohydrates of which sugars	44.6g 0.9g	9.9g 0.2g
Fat of which saturates	12.2g 6.1g	2.7g 1.4g
Fibre	3.2g	0.7g
Sodium	1.0g	0.2g

A serving (450g) contains the equivalent of approx **2.5g of salt.**

Guideline daily amounts			
Each day	Women	Men	Per serving
Calories	2000	2500	387
Fat	70.0g	95.0g	12.2g
Salt	5.0g	7.0g	2.5g

These figures are for average adults of normal weight. Your own requirements will vary with age, size and activity level.

The first thing to look for is:
- Serving size: Check the stated serving size. When you are comparing brands of any type of food, make sure you are comparing the same serving sizes. For example, look at each per 100g.
- Calories (kcals): Obviously, if you are intending to lose weight, then this is a key criterion in your selection of brands. Calories are usually refereed to as kcals on labels. Again, when you are comparing brands, this is the first item to check, as it often flags up possible problems with fat and sugar levels.

- Fat: Here we are looking for low-fat brands, e.g. Tesco Healthy Living, but, more importantly, those with the lowest saturated fat levels. Avoid products listing hydrogenated oils or trans fats.
- Fibre: this is really critical in the low Gi programme as the Gi of foods is significantly affected by its fibrous content. Fibrous foods have a lower Gi so, when you are comparing brands, look for those with higher fibre levels.
- Salt: Salt has a major impact on blood pressure. If you have any major risk factors for heart disease and stroke, such as being overweight, having high blood pressure (*hypertension*), or a genetic predisposition to these, then you should pay close attention to the sodium or salt content.
- Sugar: Again, if losing weight is your main concern, sugar levels are important to watch.

BEST BUY

So, if you are interested in a healthy diet that will let you lose weight at the same time, look on the label for brands that have:

- low Gi rating (see Gi food lists on pages 119–38)
- low sugar levels*
- lower fat content, particularly saturated fats
- higher fibre levels*
- and, if you are at risk of heart disease or stroke, then look for low salt (sodium) brands.

*The Food Standards Authority (FSA) offers 'Rules of Thumb' to judge if products have a lot or a little of a particular nutrient. The commonest are based on a per 100g measurement and are as follows:

	A LOT	A LITTLE		A LOT	A LITTLE
Fat	20g	3g	Sugars	10g	2g
Saturates	5g	1g	Salt	1.25g	0.25g

RICK'S RECOMMENDED SERVING SIZES FOR DIETING

FOODS	PORTION RECOMMENDED
Low Gi breads (which have at least 2½–3g fibre per slice)	1 slice
Low Gi cereals	60g (2oz)
Nuts	8–10
Margarine (non-hydrogenated, low-fat)	2 tsp
Meat, seafood, poultry (the size of a pack of cards)	120g (4oz)
Olive/rapeseed oil	1 tsp
Olives	4–5
Pasta	40g (1⅓oz) uncooked
Potatoes (boiled, new)	2–3
Rice (long grain, basmati)	50g (1¼oz) uncooked

PORTIONS AND SERVING SIZES

Another big advantage of eating the low Gi way is that, with a few exceptions, there are no recommended serving sizes. This is not a deprivation diet. For the most part you can eat as much of the low Gi foods as you like. There are a few exceptions – those that have a higher fat or calorie content, which are listed below. What is required is a large dose of common sense so you don't start eating twelve apples a day or a litre of low-fat yoghurt at one sitting. We don't recommend that you go overboard on quantities of anything. Moderation is the keyword.

Two-step plan

In Rick Gallop's *The Gi Diet*, he has developed two steps or phases in his weight-control programme:

STEP 1

This is the weight-loss period when you will lose those pounds painlessly without going hungry and feeling deprived. Here you will focus on low Gi foods that are also low in fat and sugar. This doesn't mean you can't have the occasional fling. Falling off the wagon, while not encouraged, is acceptable, as this diet is not a straitjacket. Try to eat the low Gi way 90% of the time and you will be doing fine. The occasional lapse at worst will only delay you achieving your target weight level by a week or two.

STEP 2

This is the maintenance phase and how you will eat for the rest of your life! Here you are encouraged to add more medium Gi foods to your diet and you may increase the above serving sizes by up to 50%. This is also a time to reward yourself for achieving your target weight by adding some of the forbidden foods such as 70% cocoa chocolate or a glass of wine (preferably red) with your dinner. Wine has been demonstrated to be beneficial to heart health but do not make the assumption that, if one glass is good for you, two will be even better and so on! One glass per day is your best option.

A word of warning. By this time your new leaner body will require fewer calories to function as you have less weight to carry around, and it has also learned how to use calories more efficiently while you've been reducing your calorie input. So you don't need to make any significant changes to your diet to maintain your new weight. Just stick to low and medium Gi foods that are low in fat, particularly saturated fat, and sugar.

One of the amazing benefits you will feel with your new body is your increased energy level. Not really surprising if you realise how much extra weight you used to carry around. A good way to understand this is to pack a knapsack full of books (your old diet books!) weighing about the same as the weight you have lost. Carry it around the house for an hour one evening and then put it down. That is what you have been carrying around all the time – and you can't put that down! No wonder you had no energy, sore joints and found it painful to exercise. Keep that knapsack handy and pick it up from time to time as a motivator and reminder.

HOW MUCH WEIGHT SHOULD I LOSE?

Body Mass Index

Everyone has their own particular body makeup, metabolism and genes so there are no absolute rules for how much you should weigh. The nearest to an international standard is the Body Mass Index (BMI) which measures your weight against your height. You can calculate your BMI by dividing your weight in kilograms by your height in metres squared. For example, if you weigh 60kg and you are 1.60m tall, then $60 \div (1.60 \times 1.60) = 23.4$.

If your BMI falls between 19 and 24, your weight is within the acceptable norm; 25–29 is viewed as overweight; and 30+ as obese. With a bit of extra calculation, you can work out what would be an acceptable weight for your height and that should then indicate how much weight you need to lose.

Women have a lower muscle mass and smaller frame than men, so women might want to target towards the lower end of the range while men should generally target the higher end. However, if you are under eighteen, elderly or muscle-bound these ratings do not apply to you. For those over 65, we suggest you allow an extra 4.5kg (10lb) to help protect you in case of a fall or as an extra energy reserve should you suffer a long debilitating illness.

As we've said before, use this only as a guide not as an absolute number. Nevertheless, it's a good general measure and the only one that has been accepted as an international standard.

Waist measurement

The other measurement you should concern yourself with is your waist measurement. This is an even better predictor of your health than is your weight. Abdominal fat is more than just an added weight problem. Recent research has shown that abdominal fat acts almost like a separate organ in the body, but this 'organ' is destructive – it releases harmful proteins and free fatty acids into the rest of the body and this can increase your risk of heart disease, stroke, cancer and diabetes. Doctors describe people with abdominal fat as apple-shaped.

If you are female and have a waist measurement of 88cm+ (32in+), or male with a waist measurement of 93cm (37in+), you are at risk of endangering your health. If this measurement is 93cm+ (35in+) for women and 100cm+ (40in+) for men, then you are at serious risk of heart disease, stroke, many cancers and diabetes.

To measure your waist put a tape measure around your waist at navel level till it fits snugly and is not cutting into your flesh. Do not adopt the walk-down-the-beach-suck-in-your-tummy routine! Just stand naturally. There's no point in trying to fudge the numbers because the only person you're kidding is yourself.

HOW LONG SHOULD IT TAKE?

This is inevitably the question that follows 'How much should I lose?'

If you are planning to lose up to 10% of your body weight (e.g. you weigh 63.6kg [10 stones] and want to lose 6.3kg [1 stone]) then you should plan on losing an average of 450g (1lb) per week. We say average, because you never lose weight in a straight line. The pattern is to lose weight more quickly at the start of the diet, followed by a series of drops and plateaus. The closer you get to your target weight, the slower your weight loss. So for a 6.3kg (1 stone) loss assume about fourteen weeks.

If you have more than 10% to lose, the good news is that you will lose more than 450g (1lb) on average a week. This is simply because your larger body requires more calories just to keep operating than someone who is lighter. For example, Mary weighs 95.4kg (15 stones) with a BMI of 34 and requires about 2700 calories a day just to keep her body operating. Jane, who is the same height but weighs 70kg (11 stones) with a BMI of 26, only needs 2000 calories per day. A typical calorie level for a low Gi diet is 1500 calories per day. So Mary will be reducing her calorie intake by 1200 calories per day, which equals a weight loss of over 1kg (2½lb) per week. Jane on the other hand has a shortfall of only 500 calories per day, which equals a weight loss of 450g (1lb) per week.

These are only approximate figures but will give you some idea of what you should expect.

SUMMARY

1. Record your current weight and waist measurements. Set a target weight. Try the knapsack test.

2. Clear the larder and fridge of all high GI foods and replace with low GI foods. (See Chapter 3 Shopping.)

3. Only eat low GI products that are low in fat, especially saturated and trans fat, and low in sugar as in Step 1.

4. Try and increase the amount of exercise you do, especially after you have lost a few pounds and find that you can exercise more with your lighter body and higher energy levels. Make this an integral part of your daily life not as an optional add-on. See Chapter 6 for inspiration.

5. Go for it!

3 Shopping

Now that you are convinced that eating the low Gi way is the way to go, you can't wait to get to your nearest Tesco – but, before you set out with your book and shopping list in hand, there are a couple of preliminary steps:

• Clear out the pantry. Almost certainly your pantry and fridge will contain a selection of high Gi foods. So to make a clean break with your unhealthy past and to avoid future temptations, clear them out! If the thought of throwing them in the dustbin makes you feel guilty, then donate them to your local charity or skinny neighbours. It will be a clear sign to the family that changes are on the way and everyone will soon be eating in a new, healthy and nutritious way.

• Eat before you shop. One of the worst mistakes you can make is to go shopping on an empty stomach. The result will be that you will be more tempted to buy those high Gi, fat- and sugar-rich foods, however good your original intentions. The first few times you shop the low Gi way will require a little more time and concentration. It is not a time to be distracted by an empty tummy. Soon it will become second nature and your new eating patterns will be well established – you will be less likely to be distracted by hunger pangs. If you're eating the low Gi way, then hunger pangs in any case will be a thing of the past!

You have now arrived at Tesco with your shopping list and book in hand with a full stomach. We propose to take you section by section through the store giving you some guidelines for making the right Gi choices.

All of the low Gi foods listed in this chapter are also low in saturated fat and calories. If you want to lose or control your weight, then these are your best choices.

Vegetables

Vegetables are a low Gi wonderland. Virtually all vegetables are low Gi and high in fibre, nutrients, minerals and vitamins. The only general exceptions are root vegetables (check listings on page 118). They also count towards your '5-a-day' target. As we discussed earlier, cooking raises the Gi of foods and it also reduces some of the nutrient content. So try eating them raw with a tasty low-fat dip as a snack; if you do need to cook them, use as little water as possible and undercook – microwaving is excellent for preparing vegetables.

Remember cooking is the first step in the digestive process of breaking down food. The more processing that goes on outside your body, the less your digestive system is left to do. And, as we discussed earlier, the more processing your body has to do, the better. Keeping your digestive system busy means it is not looking for its next meal!

Just look at the incredible range of vegetables that are available at Tesco from all over the world. Unfortunately most of us limit our choices to a narrow selection. So break with tradition, live a little and choose some that you've never tried before.

The only vegetables that have a medium or high Gi are certain root vegetables such as potatoes, turnips and beetroot. If you are trying to lose weight, avoid these in Step 1. The main exceptions are carrots and new potatoes. As we discussed on page 17, it is the *type* of potato that you eat and *how you prepare* it. Your best bet is boiled small new potatoes.

Fruits

FRESH

Virtually all fresh fruits are low Gi and also count towards your '5-a-day' target. A few exceptions are those with particularly high sugar and low fibre levels, which digest quickly resulting in a high Gi rating. Melons are a good example of this.

Fruits are an excellent source of fibre, vitamins and minerals all of which are essential for good health. They should form a cornerstone of your diet.

FROZEN, BOTTLED, CANNED, DRIED

As fresh fruits and vegetables can be expensive out of season, then your next best option is frozen. Frozen foods have virtually the same nutritional value as fresh fruit and, when bought in bulk, can be reasonably inexpensive.

Bottled and canned foods are a less advantageous choice as the bottling/canning process requires high temperatures to avoid spoilage. This not only destroys some of the nutritional value but also raises the Gi of the fruit. If you do buy canned fruit or vegetables, always drain off the water or juice first.

Many dried fruits are red light as they are very high in sugar. However, dried apricots, cranberries, apples and prunes are yellow light. All dried fruits are acceptable in modest quantities as baking ingredients to enhance flavour.

JUICES

The golden rule is to eat the fruit rather than drink the juice. The whole fruit has a lower Gi, fewer calories and more fibre and nutrition than the processed juice. Though the traditional breakfast orange juice can be a hard habit to break, it's worth doing.

Meat, soya, poultry, seafood, mycoprotein

MEAT/SOYA

Most meats contain fat, especially saturated (bad) fat, so it's important to select meats that have had all the visible fat trimmed and that are also intrinsically lean, e.g. Healthy Living Chicken. Simply trimming visible fat can reduce the amount of fat by an average of 50%. Round or loin cuts are the best for a lean choice. Processed meats such as salami are high in fat, sodium and nitrates, and are not your best choices.

Soya-based foods such as tofu, mycoprotein (e.g. Quorn) and TVP (textured vegetable protein) are high in protein, low in saturated fat and are good for a healthy heart. An excellent choice whether you are vegetarian or not.

Remember, the serving size is 120g (4oz) or about the size of a pack of cards or the palm of your hand.

POULTRY – CHICKEN AND TURKEY (WITHOUT SKIN)

The traditional benchmark for low-fat protein is skinless chicken or turkey breast. Skin removal is critical with all poultry. Dark meat (thigh, leg), duck and goose are higher in saturated fat.

In Step 1 (weight-loss phase) skinless chicken and turkey should be your preferred source of protein. They are relatively inexpensive and can be prepared in a variety of interesting ways from stir-fries to chicken salads.

SEAFOOD

All fish and shellfish are excellent choices. Here is an opportunity to explore the wonderful world of seafood outside the traditional family favourites: salmon and tuna. There is a wide variety available at Tesco from the fish counter or in pre-packaged form. One caution, seafood that is breaded or battered is not your best choice.

From a health standpoint oily fish, such as salmon, mackerel or trout, is rich in omega-3, an oil that is beneficial against heart disease and stroke. Shellfish is not the cholesterol villain that it was once thought to be.

Cereal grains

Whole grains with all the nutrition and fibre intact are, in general, low Gi, but remember that rice is one of the grains where the Gi can range from high to low. Basmati and long grain rice are good choices. Brown and wild rice, although usually more expensive, are an even better choice, as they are less processed and contain more nutrients and fibre. However, short grain rice that is glutinous and sticks together (similar to that served in Chinese restaurants or the Italian risotto rice) is not recommended.

Sugars/sweeteners/fruit spreads

Sugar and derivatives such as golden syrup and brown sugar are all high Gi.

SWEETENERS

The better choice is to go for one of the latest sweeteners, some of which are based on sugar (sucralose) and measure by volume exactly as sugar. There are several safe excellent sugar substitutes on the market and they have been approved by all Western government health agencies. If you are sensitive to aspartame, there are other excellent choices.

FRUIT SPREADS

These can be used as straightforward spreads on bread/toast or can be used as flavour enhancers with cereals, porridge and low-fat dairy products such as yoghurt, sour cream and cottage cheese.

Your best choices are spreads that contain extra fruit and low amounts of added sugar or preferably none. The clue is in the product contents listings on the label. If sugar is the first ingredient then this is not your best choice if you're trying to lose weight.

Beans (legumes)

Beans (or legumes) are almost the perfect food. Rich in protein, fibre and low in fat, they are a star in the low Gi food listings. Soya beans in particular are valuable to vegetarians as a source of protein and are very heart healthy.

Fresh, frozen or dried beans are your best choice. Canned beans can have a Gi up to 50% higher because of the high temperatures used in the canning process to avoid spoilage. However, they still fall into the low to moderate Gi range albeit at the higher end. Watch out for beans with added meat, sugar or molasses. These are not your best choices. Make beans a priority in your low Gi shopping list.

Condiments/seasonings
Most condiments are low Gi. Watch out on the ingredients list for sugar or other natural sweeteners such as honey and brown sugar. Ketchup and brown sauce have high sugar content, so use them sparingly.

Fats/oils/dressings
Fat is an essential part of a healthy diet. The issue is eating the right type of fat. (See pages 9–10.)

The good fats and oils are vegetable-based and the gold star award goes to rapeseed oil and olive oil. These should be your preferred choices.

Dressings should be low fat. You can make your own simple low Gi dressing by squeezing the juice of a lemon onto your meal.

As acid reduces the Gi level of a meal, in that it slows the digestive process, vinaigrette dressing makes an ideal choice.

Nuts and seeds
Nuts and seeds are an excellent source of good fats and protein. Some nuts have more monosaturated (best) fat than others. Remember that all nuts are calorie dense so limit your quantities (typically 8–10 nuts per serving). It is very easy to sit in front of the

TV and consume quite unconsciously a bowl of nuts which, incidentally, equals your total calorie needs for an entire day!

While 100% nut butters, such as peanut butter, have a low Gi and contain good fats, they are very high in calories so should be used in very limited quantities. If you can restrain yourself to 1 tablespoon, you can have this as an occasional treat in Step 1. Only 100% peanut brands qualify, as other versions contain fillers such as sugar, starches or hydrogenated oils.

Pasta

Most durum wheat pastas are low to medium Gi, especially the wholemeal variety. Just watch the quantity (a maximum of 100g /4oz – or, as Rick recommends, 40g/1⅓oz, if dieting – uncooked) and always slightly undercook – *al dente*. All pastas with cheese or meat fillings or which are pre-packaged or tinned are not good choices if you are trying to lose weight.

PASTA SAUCES

Tomato paste sauces that are low in sugar are the best choice. Tomato sauce is also rich in lycopene, which has been shown to reduce the risk of prostate cancer.

Snacks

For those trying to lose weight we recommend three snacks a day, so this is an important section, but loaded with aisles of temptation!

Fortunately there are many excellent choices ranging from low-fat dairy products to nutrition (cereal) bars (see next page), fruit and nuts.

Soups

Soups are useful for reducing the amount of food you eat during the rest of the meal. Look for chunky vegetable-based soups and avoid cream-based soups. Most canned soups have a higher Gi than soups made from scratch because of the high processing temperatures needed to avoid spoilage. So if you have the time, it is best to make your own. There are a couple of delicious recipes on pages 89 and 97.

Breakfast foods

CEREALS

Many breakfast cereals are high Gi. They are made from highly processed grains, which lack both nutrition and fibre. Beware of those so-called healthy granola type of cereals (those that appear to be made up of healthy clusters of grains and nuts), which are usually low in fibre and high in sugar.

The exceptions are cereals made with at least 10g of fibre per serving. While they are not in themselves much fun, they are easily dressed up into tasty dishes by topping them, for example, with nuts, flaxseed, fruit and Healthy Living Natural Yoghurt.

The king of hot cereals is porridge, made with large flake oats (traditional variety, not instant or quick). It takes about three minutes in the microwave and, along with toppings such as fruit, sliced almonds/ground flaxseed or fruit yoghurt, will make a delicious start to your day.

CEREAL BARS

Do not be misled by the recent flood of breakfast bars that appear to burst with health. These are high in processed cereals and sugar, and low in fibre. They are not a good choice if you are trying to lose weight. If you are in an unavoidable rush at breakfast time, it's better to go for a Tesco Healthy Eating nutrition bar with more protein and fibre and less sugar. They are strictly an exception, not the rule. Breakfast is the pivotal meal of the day.

PANCAKES/WAFFLES

Packaged pancake mixers and frozen waffles are high Gi. However, you can make your own pancakes, crepes and French toast from scratch yourself. See recipes in *Living the Gi Diet* (Virgin Books).

Beverages
See Chapter 2 (page 24).

Dairy foods
Low-fat dairy products are a low Gi staple. They are rich in protein, calcium and vitamin D. Regular dairy foods are not recommended as the fat is mainly saturated (bad) fat. Butter and cheese are amongst the principal villains.

Fruit-flavoured, fat-free yoghurts with a sweetener are ideal for adding to breakfast cereals, as a snack or as a topping on fruit for dessert.

Full-flavoured cheeses such as mature cheddar, feta and Stilton are acceptable in limited quantities as a flavour enhancer; for example, when sprinkled lightly on salads, omelettes and pasta. There is also a a variety of tasty reduced fat cheeses in the Healthy Living range, as well as a heart-healthy cholesterol reducing cheese.

Soya milk is increasingly popular and a good choice if you are lactose intolerant or allergic to dairy products. There are many more gluten-, wheat- and dairy-free products in the Free From Tesco range.

With soya milk look for plain, low-fat versions with added calcium as the flavoured ones can contain high levels of sugar.

Bread
Interpreting nutritional labelling on breads needs some practice. That healthy-looking seven-grain wholesome loaf may be, on closer

inspection, not be what it purports to be. There are two clues: the flour and fibre.

If your seven-grain loaf lists unbleached or enriched white flour as the first ingredient, then most of the bran, fibre and nutrients have been stripped out. The first ingredient should read 100% wholemeal or wholegrain flour. If it is stone-ground, which produces a coarser flour, even better.

Fibre content should be a minimum of 2.5–3g per slice. It's the combination of whole grains with fibre that delivers a lower Gi bread.

Other breads that traditionally have been associated with weight loss, such as crispbreads, are low in fibre and have a high Gi. However, the latest high-fibre crispbreads are much more acceptable. Look for at least 2g of fibre per slice.

All breads that are made principally from white flour (or 'enriched' flour) including bagels, croissants, baguettes and crumpets are high Gi and not recommended if weight control is your concern. Good choices are granary and multigrain bread.

SUMMARY

1. Clear out the pantry of red-light foods.

2. Eat before you shop.

3. Low Gi foods that are low in fat (particularly saturated fat) and sugar are your best choices.

4. Eat lean meat only.

5. The less processed your food is, the better it is for your body.

6. Try to keep to monosaturated or polyunsaturated fats in your diet.

7. The best breakfast is porridge.

4 Practical tips

By now you know how the Glycaemic Index works and how it can let you lose weight and keep it off. You may even have started and are delighted to see those pounds disappearing, your waistline shrinking and the excitement in dropping a dress or trouser size or two. But, whether you're starting, already into the programme or moving to weight maintenance in Step 2, you are bound to face the inevitable dieting hurdles that test everyone's firmest resolve. Food cravings, festive holidays, celebrations, vacations and 'falling off the wagon' are all challenges to healthy eating. Here are some practical tips to deal with these dietary hazards.

Food cravings
What makes losing weight particularly challenging is that we tend to enjoy and desire fattening foods such as chocolate, biscuits, ice cream, peanut butter, chips and so on. The most important thing to remember about cravings is that we're only human and it's natural to succumb to temptation every now and then. Don't feel guilty about it. If you 'cheat', you aren't totally blowing your diet. You're simply experiencing a temporary blip in your good eating habits. If you have a small piece of chocolate cake after dinner, or perhaps a beer with your friend while watching a match, make sure you savour the extravagance by eating or drinking slowly. Really enjoy it. Then get back on track in the morning with a low Gi breakfast and stick to the straight and narrow for the next couple of weeks. You will continue to lose weight, and that's what it's all about.

However, eating the low Gi way will help prevent lapses in two key ways.
• First, you will find that, after you've been on the programme for a few weeks, you will have developed a built-in warning system: you

won't feel good physically when you eat too many high Gi food because your blood sugar will spike and crash. You'll feel bloated, uncomfortable and lethargic, and you may even get a headache – a strong deterrent against straying into high Gi territory.
• Second, because you are eating three meals and three snacks daily, you won't feel hungry between meals. If you skip any, you will probably start longing for forbidden foods – so make sure that you eat all the recommended meals and snacks every day.

Despite the diet's built-in security system, there will be times when a craving gets the better of you. What should you do? Well, you could try substituting a low Gi food for the high Gi food you're thinking about. If you want something sweet, try having fruit; apple purée; low-fat yoghurt with sweetener; low-fat ice cream with no added sugar; any of the dessert recipes (see page 95); a nutrition bar or a caffeine-free diet soft drink. If what you want is something salty and crunchy, try having celery sticks with Healthy Living Cream Cheese. Your craving for chocolate in Step 1 may be alleviated with a chocolate-flavoured nutrition bar. As you can see, there are many lower Gi versions of the foods we normally reach for when a craving strikes.

Holidays and celebrations
Birthdays, Christmas, Easter and so on all have one thing in common: an abundance of food. Holidays are generally centred around traditional feasts and dishes. But, even so, you don't have to throw the Gi guidelines out the window. You can eat the low Gi way and still have a fun and festive holiday. If you host the event yourself, you will be able to decide what type of food is served. Think of what you would normally eat during the holiday and look for low Gi alternatives.

For example, if you usually have a roast turkey with bread-based stuffing for Christmas, have a roast turkey with wild or basmati rice stuffing instead. If you always make cranberry sauce with sugar, prepare it with a sugar substitute. There is no shortage of low Gi vegetables to serve as side dishes, and dessert could be elegant poached pears or a pavlova with berries. You can put on a completely low Gi feast without your guests even realising.

If you celebrate the holiday at someone else's home, you will obviously have less control over the menu. You could help out the busy host by offering to bring a vegetable side dish or the dessert – a low Gi one of course. Once seated at the holiday table, survey the dishes and try to compose your plate as you would at home: vegetables on half the plate, rice or pasta on one quarter and protein on the other quarter. Pass on the bread rolls and mashed potatoes – have extra vegetables instead. If you wish, you can allow yourself a concession by having a small serving of dessert. If you aren't particularly big on sweets, you might prefer to have a glass of wine instead. Try not to indulge in both.

Cocktail parties can also be fun, low Gi occasions. Instead of alcohol, you can have a fruit-juice-based cocktail, a glass of mineral water with a twist of lemon or a diet caffeine-free soft drink. If you really would like an alcoholic beverage, have only one and choose the healthiest option. Red wine is your best bet, or a white wine spritzer made half with wine and half with sparkling water. Be sure to consume any alcohol with food to slow down the rate at which you metabolise it.

Before you go have a low Gi meal or snack such as a bowl of low Gi cereal with fruit or Healthy Eating yoghurt before you go so you won't be tempted to eat too much. Then choose the low Gi appetisers and enjoy your time with friends and family.

Holidays

Just because you are on holiday doesn't mean you shouldn't continue to eat three meals and three snacks daily. In your suitcase, pack some low Gi snacks to take with you, such as nutrition bars, nuts and any other non-perishables. Once there, you can buy non-fat, sugar-free yoghurt, fruit, low-fat cottage cheese to snack on. If you are driving to your destination or are going on a road trip, your only option along the motorway may be fast food. If you can, pack some low Gi meals and snacks to take with you, so you won't have to stop to eat. Otherwise, we have provided some tips for eating at fast-food outlets on page 70.

Falling off the wagon

This is without doubt everyone's major concern and it doesn't need to be. As we stated before, this diet is not a straitjacket. If you can be on the programme for 90% of the time that's just fine. The worst that can happen is that you will delay reaching your weight target by a week or two. This is a real-world way of eating that recognises the realities of social and time pressures, eating on the run and the sheer temptation to binge on occasion. Again, as with food cravings, the Gi plan has a built-in warning signal when you go off the rails. After a few weeks eating the low Gi way, keeping your blood sugar levels steady, your body will react with alarm to any sudden onslaught of high Gi foods as your blood sugar soars and then plummets leaving you bloated, tired and irritable. It will be a relief to climb back on board the low Gi wagon.

Plateauing

The most important thing to recognise is that you do not lose weight in a straight line but rather with a series of starts and stops. This results in hitting a plateau of a week or even two or three weeks when nothing seems to happen. Sound familiar?

As we mentioned earlier, the average weight-loss target is 450g (1lb) per week if you have approximately 10% of your body weight to lose. If you have more than 10% of your body weight to lose, then you will lose weight at a faster rate. So someone who weighs 114.5kg (18 stones) and wishes to lose 32kg (5 stones) (30%) will probably lose an average of around 900g to 1.3kg (2–3lb) a week.

So what you should do is count the number of weeks you have been eating the low Gi way and divide them into the pounds lost. This will give you your average weekly weight loss, which you will find almost invariably hits your objective. This means you're on target and don't fret as your weight loss *will* start again.

If you are falling behind on your average or the plateau lasts more than a couple of weeks, then you need to check the serving sizes of your low Gi foods. Look specifically at serving sizes on the products that have been specified in this book, such as potatoes, pasta, rice and nuts (see page 28). Check you are following the guidelines.

With all other low Gi products make sure moderation is your motto. Be honest with yourself and review what you are currently eating.

Getting the family involved

There are many advantages to having the whole family eat the low Gi way. First, this is a healthy, nutritious diet for the whole family to follow. Second, for those members of the family who need to lose weight the advantages are obvious. Third, if you want to avoid cooking three separate meals, then having the whole family eating the same way is clearly the route to go.

SPOUSE/PARTNER

Getting your partner or spouse eating the low Gi way is important as it's great to have mutual support and encouragement. If you have children, then you both represent key role models for how to eat.

The best approach is to sit down and discuss with your partner your desire to change the way you eat. Point out that, whether or not your partner needs to lose weight, the change to a Gi diet is a healthier way of eating that will provide more energy and reduce the risk of major diseases such as diabetes, heart disease, stroke and cancer. Simply go to Step 2 of the programme for your partner if weight is not an issue, which means adding a few more choices to their menu and some adjustment to serving sizes.

However, as over half the UK population is overweight, there is an odds-on chance that your partner has some pounds to lose. If you prepare the food and if your partner is reluctant to change and give up those favourite high Gi foods, then your best option is to introduce more lower Gi foods to the meals and provide tasty alternatives to their high Gi choices. This is exactly what you will find in the delicious recipes in the menu plans and recipes on page 81.

You will be amazed how quickly your partner will adapt. Not only because the lower Gi choices taste great but also by eating a more nutritional diet, they actually will feel better with more energy and no after lunch/dinner slump.

For the serious objector you have two choices:

• Let your partner watch your transformation into a slimmer, more energetic and healthier you, and how people comment and ask you how you did it. Your partner will soon want to join you and emulate your success!

• Alternatively, you can try the stealth method. Simply adjust the menu and say nothing.

One reader who went on *The Gi Diet* began serving herself and her husband low Gi meals for dinner every night without telling him they were based on the Gi guidelines. He never even realised he was eating according to the recommendations of a diet plan until he had to have his trousers taken in!

CHILDREN

A child's daily nutritional intake affects every aspect of their life. Their behaviour, mood, energy, performances at school and susceptibility to infection and diseases are all affected by what they eat. Many other behaviour issues such as attention deficit disorder could often be better addressed by diet than by the quick-fix drugs that are all too readily used.

Do not put children under five years on a low Gi diet – they have specific nutritional needs in their early development. For further information on feeding this age group consult your doctor.

The low Gi diet rich in fruit, vegetables, whole grains, low-fat dairy and meat, nuts and legumes is ideal for healthy growing children. Just make sure they are getting plenty of good fats in their diet as they are essential for growing bodies. But, as this is perhaps a far cry from how they are currently eating, the question inevitably is: will they co-operate?

This is further complicated by the dynamics of family relationships, which are frequently acted out at mealtimes. It is one of the few areas where a child has a sense of control by choosing to eat or not. At the same time mothers consider nutrition and food preparation as a key responsibility to their family. Parental control and children's autonomy are set for a collision and I doubt there is a parent alive who has not experienced this.

Rely rather on the child's inherent survival instinct to determine hunger and appetite. Believe it or not, children will eat and are quite capable of regulating their own food intake. They generally have an aversion to new foods, which stems from primitive times when experimenting with new foods could be fatal. However, they will accept them eventually given sufficient exposure and time.

Perversely, the more you try to cajole or force food on children the more likely they are to develop resistance to eating. Similarly, if they feel deprived, they will have a tendency to overeat. So step back, relax, focus on positive parenting and examine your own food behaviours. Your own behaviour as a role model will have the greatest impact on your child's relationship with food.

The phrase 'Do as I do, not do as I say' could never be more appropriate than when you are trying to get children to eat the right foods. Too often children are excluded from food shopping, meal selection or food preparation. There is no reason why this should be the case except parental reluctance to complicate their lives! The most important recommendation is to engage your children in this new venture to get them involved. Explain why and how the family has decided to eat the low Gi way. Rather than focusing on weight management, talk about this being a nutritious way of eating aimed at improving the family's health and lifestyle. This is the way the family is going to eat from here on.

Make this a big adventure and encourage them to be an active part of it. Remind them that we have a health crisis on our hands mainly because of how we eat. Show them the Gi food ratings and you'll be amazed by how quickly they catch on to how it works.

While it is not always practical, the occasional foray with the children to Tesco is a good idea, as they have an opportunity to learn firsthand how and why you make food choices. It's an educational opportunity to help your children understand how to make their own healthy choices. It all starts here.

SUMMARY

1. If you are tempted to eat a high-Gi food, don't feel guilty. Get back on track the next day.

2. Try substituting a high-Gi snack with a low-Gi one.

3. At parties and celebratory meals, try keeping to one unit of alcohol, and compose your plate as you would at home.

4. Pack your own lower-Gi snacks when travelling.

5. Plateauing may be due to your portion size creeping up.

6. Get the family involved.

5 Health and reducing the risk of disease

The most alarming medical news about fat, which runs contrary to conventional wisdom, is that it's not (as previously thought) a passive accumulator of energy reserves and extra baggage. Rather it is an active, living part of your body. In fact, it behaves very much like any of our other body organs such as the liver, heart or kidney once it has formed sufficient mass. But the beer belly, saddle or love handles undermine your body's health by pumping out a dangerous combination of free fatty acids and proteins. This causes out-of-control cell division and proliferation, which is directly associated with the growth of malignant cancer tumours. It also creates inflammation, which is linked to atherosclerosis, the principal cause of heart disease and stroke. And if that wasn't bad enough, they also increase insulin resistance leading to type II diabetes. In fact, these fat tissues have many characteristics of a huge tumour and that thought might help encourage many fence sitters to start doing something about that weight.

Foods are, in effect, drugs. They have a powerful influence on our health, wellbeing and emotional state. We take in food four or five times a day, usually with more thought for taste than for nutritional value. It would be incomprehensible to take drugs on the same basis. The right foods can help you maintain your health, extend your life span, give you more energy and make you feel good and sleep better. Couple that with exercise and you are doing all you can to keep healthy, fit and alert. The rest is a matter of genes and luck. Let's take a quick look at the importance of diet, not in fact just managing our weight, but as a critical factor in preventing diseases.

DIABETES

A significant benefit of eating a low Gi diet is its impact on people who either suffer from type II diabetes or are at risk of developing type II diabetes stems from the body's inability to utilise insulin to remove excess glucose from the bloodstream. The result is a build-up of glucose in the blood (*hyperglycaemia*) which, if not checked, will ultimately kill the individual.

So control of blood sugar levels is key to the management of diabetes. That is why a low Gi diet is so important for people with type II diabetes and those at risk. Lower Gi foods help keep the blood sugars under control by keeping them within the normal range. Keeping levels in the range helps prevent further complications such as heart disease, stroke, kidney failure and even amputations.

Being overweight and lacking exercise are two of the principal factors that contribute towards diabetes. So, whether you already have diabetes or have been diagnosed at risk, your best chance to minimise medication or avoid it altogether is to lose weight, exercise more and eat a low Gi diet. An additional advantage of eating the low Gi way is that this will not only help you manage your blood sugar levels but will also help you lose weight. The research evidence is overwhelming.

As there is no cure for diabetes yet, prevention is by far your best option. This is one of the most preventable diseases and you have every opportunity and all the knowledge to do something about it. So get right into your low Gi eating and exercise plan and get those pounds off.

Interestingly, more people with diabetes die of heart disease than diabetes in part because the principal controllable risk factors – overweight, lacking exercise and diet – are all the same. This makes an appropriate bridge to our next disease, heart disease and stroke.

HEART DISEASE AND STROKE

Heart disease and stroke are the cause of 40% of all deaths. It's been calculated that, if we led even a moderate lifestyle (reduced our weight, exercised regularly and quit smoking), we could halve the carnage from these diseases. Though heart disease, like most cancers, is primarily a disease of old age, nearly half of those who suffer heart attacks are under the age of 65.

With regard to diet, the simple fact is that the fatter you are the more likely it is you will suffer a heart attack or stroke. The two key factors that link heart disease and stroke to diet are blood cholesterol and hypertension.

Hypertension

High blood pressure is the early warning light for both heart disease and stroke. High blood pressure puts more stress on the arterial system and causes it to age and deteriorate more rapidly, ultimately leading to arterial damage, blood clots and heart attack or stroke. Excess weight has a major bearing on high blood pressure.

Cholesterol

Cholesterol is essential to your body's metabolism. However, high blood levels are a problem, as cholesterol is the key ingredient in the plaque that can build up in your arteries, eventually cutting off the blood supply to your heart (causing heart attack) or your brain (leading to stroke). To make things more complicated, there are two forms of cholesterol: HDL (good) cholesterol and LDL (bad) cholesterol. The idea is to boost the HDL level while depressing the LDL level.

Remember it this way: HDL is 'Heart's Delight Level' and LDL is 'Leads to Death Level'!

The villain that raises LDL levels is saturated fat. Conversely, polyunsaturated and monounsaturated fats not only lower LDL levels but also actually boost HDL. The moral: make sure some fat is included in your diet, but make sure it's the right fat. (Refer to Chapter 1 for the complete lowdown on fat.)

CANCER

There is increasing evidence that weight and diet are critical risk factors for most forms of cancer. Diets high in animal fats (saturated), such as some of today's high-protein diets, are directly associated with increased risk of breast, uterine, colon and prostate cancers.

We talked earlier about the 'beer belly' and its stimulation of cell division, which can lead to malignant tumours. Breast cancer death rates, for instance, for obese postmenopausal women are 50% higher than for women of normal weight, and obese men are twice as likely to develop colon cancer as men of normal weight.

At a recent meeting of leading cancer researchers, one of the key recommendations for reducing the risk of cancer was that individuals should choose a diet that includes a variety of vegetables, fruits and whole grains – the low Gi diet in a nutshell.

ALZHEIMER'S DISEASE

Over the past two to three years there has been a steady flow of research studies all linking Alzheimer's and diet. There appears to be a clear correlation with high saturated fat, which doubles the risk of getting this dreadful disease. Alcohol, salt and high Gi carbs are also associated.

On the plus side, a diet rich in deep-sea fish (i.e. oily fish), such as salmon, mackere and, sardines, significantly reduces your risk. It is suggested that omega-3 oil and vitamin E found in these fish are the key agents.

The low Gi diet, low in saturated fat and rich in omega-3 and vitamin E, is your best defence against Alzheimer's and other dementias.

ARTHRITIS

Again diet appears to have a distinct correlation with managing arthritis and, especially osteoarthritis, in a couple of ways. First, being overweight and/or obese puts a severe strain on joints especially the weight-bearing ones. Knee, hip or ankle may be taking on an extra 22.5–27kg (50–60lb) impact each time your foot hits the ground. Try lifting a 22.5kg (50lb) weight and you'll quickly see what I mean. So get that weight off!

Second, research suggests that eating a diet that is rich in fruit, vegetables, fish (oily fish is the best), nuts, seeds, pulses and whole grains is associated with a reduction in the pain, inflammation and discomfort associated with arthritis – again the low Gi diet in a nutshell.

SUMMARY

Eat lower GI foods to help reduce your weight and help.

1. Control blood sugar levels for management and prevention of diabetes.

2. Lower cholesterol and blood pressure levels to reduce risk of heart disease and stroke.

3. Reduce saturated fats associated with cancer and Alzheimer's.

4. Reduce inflammation associated with arthritic pain.

6 Getting active

Physical activity isn't just a choice; it's an essential part of your lower Gi lifestyle – following a programme of activity can help you to lose more weight while you follow a balanced lower Gi diet. This need not be daunting. As you can see from the steps below, it is not complicated or difficult to get started. What's more, it will improve your general health and fitness as well as helping you lose weight.

WHY GET ACTIVE?

Activity is a good thing in itself – it is essential for good health and for controlling weight.

GOOD NEWS ABOUT ACTIVITY

Facilitates weight loss

Helps keep weight off

Builds muscle tone

Creates a leaner, trimmer body

Makes you feel better

Promotes a 'healthy glow'

Combats tiredness and creates feeling of more energy

Reduces blood fats

Is good fun

How does a Gi diet give you a head start with activity?

By choosing lower Gi foods you will be getting the majority of your energy from slower-releasing energy foods. So you will be able to go longer without snacking and feel 'well fuelled' and able to take part in activities after your meals. Always leave at least an hour after eating before doing any activity – 1½–2 hours is ideal. A combination

of an apple, banana and a glass of soya milk or low-fat dairy milk
2 hours before is a simple and tasty way to prepare for exercise.

GETTING STARTED

Before you start this programme, do check with your GP beforehand.
Although they will generally be very supportive, they have details
of your medical history and there may be a particular reason why
they may want to alter your activity plan. If you have diabetes, do
check with your specialist nurse, GP or dietician before you start,
as activity will decrease your blood glucose and your insulin needs
will be different.

Ten steps to a new, active you
1. Start now It does not have to be complicated to start getting active
– start right now; don't put it off until you have the right trainers, the
sky has brightened, you have lost another couple of pounds, etc –
work out a plan now and commit to it. Seize the day!
2. You are where you are Start where you are at the moment fitness-
wise, and increase the effort gradually. Remember the tortoise and
the hare. It doesn't matter where you have come from; it matters
where activity will take you. Today's walk around the park may
become a fun-run by the summer and a marathon by next year! The
Chinese have a saying for this – 'A journey of a thousand miles starts
with a single step'.
3. Do what you enjoy If walking is your thing, walk. If your ambition
is to run round the park without stopping, then walking is a great
start. Below are some simple activities to try, and there is a quick
guide to activities at the end of this chapter – have a look and you
are sure to find something that you enjoy.
• Aim for 30 minutes of moderate activity on at least five days of the

week. This may be made up of sessions of a minimum of 10 minutes duration. When you have built up your fitness, the next stage is to aim to complete three sessions of 20 minutes of more intensive activity each week.

• After following an activity plan for three weeks, keep at it, but each week try and go that bit further/faster, etc.

IDEAS FOR GETTING ACTIVE

Walk round the park

Buy a skipping rope and do as many jumps as you can in a quarter of an hour

See how far you can swim in half an hour in the local pool

Walk the dog

Challenge a friend to a knock-about on the tennis court

Book a 'Bums & Tums', Yoga or Pilates class

Hoover the house

Mow the lawn and do some gardening

Clean the car

• Try and do some of the activities above at least five times a week for a month.

4. Start your activity plan with a friend This should help keep you motivated. Buy them a copy of this book! You can share the frustrations and triumphs of your 'getting active' plan with them. Make a pact to support each other when the going gets difficult.

You could each put £1 into a box every time you exercise together and plan to spend it on a night out in a month's time!

5. Book a regular slot – time just for you Activity is important and you should feel that it is a priority over other things in life. Recruit family and friends as 'supporters' by giving you the time and space to start your plan. For instance, if you have a family, them granting you the time for activity will lead to a happier, more active you, able to do more with the children and family – everybody benefits. Don't feel guilty for having this 'me time' – improving your health is the most important change you can make.

6. Make activity part of your day Use your imagination to work some form of activity into your daily routine:

• Get off the bus a stop early and walk home.
• Walk the children to school, rather than taking the car.
• Take 30 minutes of your lunch break to walk around outside your workplace at a brisk pace.
• Cycle to work.
• Take a quick swim before you go to work.

7. Keep track of what you have done Monitor your progress. Start a diary to cover the activity you have done in the previous week, so that you can look back and see how things are developing. Make a note of what you did, how long you went for, what you enjoyed and what you didn't, and how it made you feel. It will motivate you for next time. Treat yourself to a new pair of cross-trainers or a sports top when you have finished a week/month in your diary.

8. Think of an aim or objective What goals – short and longer term – could you create for yourself that you would feel proud of? It could be completing a fun-run such as the Tesco-sponsored Cancer Research UK 10 or swimming 30 lengths non-stop. It can be anything. Focus on how you will feel when you achieve that goal, e.g. what friends, colleagues and family will say when you have achieved it. When it gets tough you can conjure up those thoughts, feelings and images to help you through the sticky patches. Remember, visualisation is one of the best ways to get where you want to be!

9. Choose the right level to exercise at, for you When you do any activity, focus on working hard enough so that you get slightly out of breath and feel your body warm up. Obviously this will vary depending on the individual. For instance, on a gentle run, you should be able to keep up a conversation at the same time. If you can't talk, you are overdoing it, and, if you can recite whole works of Shakespeare, you are not working hard enough!

10. Dress for the part Active sports involve a modest amount of kit, some of which you may already have, some of which you may need to buy. There is a wide selection at Tesco with many sports items in the Healthy Living range.

SPORTS KIT

A sports bra is essential for women. Get it fitted and make sure you wear it

A pair of good-quality trainers are invaluable – ideally cross-trainers/running trainers rather than fashion shoes

Loose-fitting activity top and 'bottoms' – ideally with stretchy and 'breathable' fabrics

A water bottle – for every 20 minutes of activity you need to drink 150ml of water, about a third of a pint

For indoor classes, an activity mat and a small hand towel are useful

The Cancer Research UK 10 – open to men and women

In 2005 Tesco will be national sponsor of the Cancer Research UK 10. Held in September and October, this is a unique fundraising series of 25 ten-kilometre runs held in the grounds of some of the UK's most beautiful stately homes. Open to both men and women of all running abilities, it is hoped that over 30,000 people will take part and help to raise £2.5 million for Cancer Research UK. This will follow on from the previous year's success where over 11,000 people ran in ten beautiful venues and raised £1 million.

Confirmed venues for 2005 include Alnwick Castle, better known as the magical 'Hogwarts School' in the *Harry Potter* films; Scone Palace in Scotland, the crowning place of the Kings of Scotland; and, for the third year running, Blenheim Palace, the birthplace of Sir Winston Churchill.

Sadly, one in three people in the UK develop cancer at some point in their life and although survival rates are improving, there are many types of cancer and many of these are still difficult to treat. Fundraising support is therefore vital in order to enable Cancer Research UK to continue to find new ways of treating and preventing cancer.

To register your interest and receive notification of when the event opens for entries please visit: www.cancerresearchuk10.co.uk

Ten ideas for fitness

Different activities can help with the appearance and strength of particular body areas. In order to see real changes you will need to do these activities three times a week, or a combination, for instance cycle a couple of times to improve your legs and also swim once a week. If you manage 20 minutes duration three times a week the gains will be quicker and you will see the results faster. Ask at your local fitness centre or gym for class details.

ACTIVITY	BENEFIT
1. Running or fast walking	General overall toning Weight loss Shape up legs Benefits the heart and lungs
2. Pilates	Improve saggy stomach muscles Control breathing Strengthen pelvic floor and lower back
3. Cycling outside or spinning on a static bike	Stamina Tone buttock and leg muscles Work at your own pace Weight loss Benefits the heart and lungs
4. Salsa	Tones the waist and hips Benefits the heart and lungs Fun and social!
5. Yoga	Gentle Improves flexibility and posture Strengthens muscles Promotes relaxation and sleep patterns
6. Swimming	Overall conditioning Non-impact – great for starting out/recovering from injury Strengthens arms and legs Benefits the heart and lungs

7. Trampolining – or mini-rebounder	Improves legs and thighs Benefits the heart and lungs
8. Hoovering/gardening/cleaning	Overall moderate intensity workout Strengthens stamina Builds arm muscles Benefits the heart and lungs
9. Skipping	Overall stamina Improves leg muscles Benefits the heart and lungs
10. Frisbee throwing	Gentle overall exercise Improves legs and thighs Stretches muscles Benefits the heart and lungs

SUMMARY

1. Eating lower GI (or slower-releasing energy) foods means that you will be able to go longer without snacking and feel 'well fuelled'.

2. Check with your doctor before embarking on an activity plan.

3. Start your exercise plan slowly, building up as you become more active.

4. Choose an exercise that you enjoy doing.

5. Join Cancer Research UK 10!

6. Try and do something for twenty minutes three times a week.

7 Eating outside the home

If you wish to manage or lose weight, one of the real challenges in eating the low Gi way is when you are eating out. Here you do not have full control over what goes into your meals but you still can make smart food choices. In this chapter we'll be dealing with some general guidelines and tips for eating out. We will be looking specifically at lunch, a time when most of us are eating out of home, fast-food and restaurant dining.

GENERAL GUIDELINES

As dining out is often a social occasion whether it be with family or with friends, it's important that you don't feel that you are a dampener on the occasion and that you are still able to enjoy yourself. Here are a few suggestions:

Eating out

1. Just before you go out, have a small bowl of high-fibre breakfast cereal (such as All-Bran) with skimmed milk or soya milk and sweetener. You could add a couple of spoons of no-fat fruit yoghurt. This will take the edge of your appetite and get some fibre into your stomach, which will help reduce the Gi of your upcoming meal.
2. On arrival, drink a glass of water which will help you feel fuller. A glass of red wine is a good idea but wait till the main course before drinking.
3. Once the habitual basket of rolls or bread has been passed round, which you ignore, ask the waiter to remove the basket as the longer it sits there the more tempted you will be to dig in.
4. Order a soup or salad first and tell the waiter you would like this as soon as possible. This will stop you sitting there hungry while others

are filling up on the bread. For soups go for vegetable or bean-based, the chunkier the better. Avoid any that are cream based. For salads, the golden rule is dressing on the side, as you will only use a fraction of what the restaurant would normally smother on – and avoid Caesar salads which usually come pre-dressed.

5. As you probably won't get boiled new potatoes and can't be sure what type of rice is being served, ask for double vegetables instead. We have yet to find a restaurant that won't willingly oblige.

6. Stick with low-fat cuts of meat or poultry where, if necessary, you can remove the skin. Fish and shellfish are an excellent choice but must not be breaded or battered. Remember, as servings tend to be generous in restaurants, eat only 4–6 oz (pack of cards size) and leave the rest.

7. As with salads, ask for any sauces to be put on the side.

8. Desserts. This is a dietary minefield with usually not a lot of low Gi choices. Fresh fruit and berries, if available, are your best choice without the ice cream. Most other choices are a dietary disaster. The best advice is to try and avoid dessert. If social pressure becomes overwhelming or it is a special occasion, ask for extra forks so the dessert can be shared. A couple of forkfuls or so along with your coffee should get you off the hook with minimal dietary damage!

9. Only order decaffeinated coffee. Skim decaf cappuccino is our family's favourite choice. Avoid liqueurs and hot chocolate.

10. Finally and perhaps most importantly, eat slowly. Try putting your fork down between mouthfuls.

The stomach can take between 20 to 30 minutes to let the brain know it feels full. So if you eat quickly, you may be shovelling in more food than you require till the brain says stop. You will also have more time to savour your meal.

What to have for lunch

Since most of us spend the lunch hour away from home, either at work, college or school, we tend to have two options for the midday meal:

• take our own, or

• eat at a restaurant.

In both cases, eating the low Gi way is definitely doable – but there are some important guidelines to keep in mind.

BRING YOUR OWN

This is really the best option for the Gi dieter. When you pack your own lunch, you can be sure that all the ingredients used are low Gi. Here are some tips for turning your regular lunch into a low Gi one.

Sandwiches This popular lunchtime mainstay is usually high Gi and high calorie. But there are several things you can do to make your sandwich low Gi. First, use one slice of 100% stone-ground wholemeal or other high-fibre bread. Spread on some mustard or hummus (no mayonnaise, butter or margarine) and top with 115g (4oz) of lean deli ham, chicken, turkey or fish. Add at least three vegetables, such as lettuce, tomato, onion or green pepper, and do not top the sandwich with another slice of bread – simply eat it open-faced. Avoid egg, chicken and tuna salad sandwiches that are made with fattening mayonnaise.

Salads Salads are almost always low Gi but are often short on protein. Add in chickpeas or other types of beans, tuna, salmon, tofu or 115g (4oz) of skinless, cooked chicken breast or other lean meat. Also watch the dressing. Use only low-fat or fat-free versions.

Soups In general, commercially canned soups have a relatively high Gi rating because of the necessary high temperatures used in the canning process. Homemade soups made with low Gi ingredients are the best option. Beware of all cream-based or puréed vegetable soups, since they are high in fat and heavily processed.

Pasta The thing to watch out for here is quantity. Your pasta dish should contain only 40g (1¹/₃oz) wholemeal pasta (dry weight), with lots of vegetables, light pasta sauce and 115g (4oz) of chicken or lean deli meat. But this still leaves you with dozens of delicious combinations.

Cottage cheese, fruit and nuts A fast and easy lunch to take to work is cottage cheese mixed with fruit and sliced almonds.

Dessert Always have some fresh fruit for dessert.

LUNCHING OUT

At a sit-down restaurant, all you have to do is order an entrée that includes a low-fat source of protein, such as chicken or fish, and vegetables. Ask for extra vegetables in place of potatoes or rice, since restaurants tend to serve the high Gi versions. For other general dining-out suggestions see the first section in this chapter.

All-you-can-eat buffets These can be your best or worst choice depending on your self-control – best, because you're free to make your own selection and there are usually lots of options for a low Gi plate; worst, because it's tempting to have a little bit of everything and then wish you'd taken a larger plate! If you're anything like us, by the time you are halfway round the buffet table, your plate is already full and you try to pile on those tantalising foods that you wished you had seen earlier. The secret is to do a quick survey of the whole buffet *before* picking up your plate and starting. Just follow the low Gi ground rules: have a look at all the options first and the buffet will definitely be your best dining-out option.

International cuisine We love trying new foods from different countries. It is a huge subject in its own right and space limitations here unfortunately do not allow for detailed recommendations.

From a low Gi standpoint your best choices are Italian, if you watch your serving sizes of pasta, and Indian, if you avoid anything deep fried. Otherwise apply the general green-light rule when choosing food and use your common sense.

Fast food For most of us fast food is a convenient and popular choice but it is full of pitfalls for the unwary. Let the following be your guide.

Up until recently it would have been really difficult to get a green-light meal at a fast-food restaurant. However, the major fast-food chains are now offering some healthy options.

The problem with most fast-food outlets is the quality and quantity of the food: you will find that hamburgers are soaked in saturated fat; fish and chicken are coated in batter or breading and then deep fried; and all the trimmings – chips, ketchup, shakes, cola – are loaded with fat and sugar. To make things even worse, everything is oversized. As food is a relatively cheap commodity in this country, doubling the hamburger, cola or chips for a few pennies more is a really attractive selling point but makes for a really bad diet. No wonder our kids are becoming obese and diabetes is prevalent.

• Salads, usually with grilled chicken, are your best choice.
• Always ask for low-fat dressings.

Other fast food Fast food-wise there is not much else better on offer. Sandwich shops are little better. We suggest that you check the menus at all fast-food outlets to see whether healthy low-Gi food is on offer. If it isn't, say why you are not buying anything – the more the customer asks or complains, the more likely the outlet is to change.

Take-away Because of our need for value for money, convenience and speed, we all use take-away outlets, but considerable caution is required. Nutrition should be our first thought, not convenience.

FISH AND CHIPS Fish and chips is the UK's most well known take-away food. However, fish and chips eaten on a regular basis can lead to obesity – they are a classic example of taking an ideal food, fish, adulterating it with calorie-loaded batter and deep-frying it in oil. Once you add the deep-fried potatoes, healthy nutrition is the last thing on your mind!

CHINESE In the main Chinese dishes are not a good choice, but if you choose carefully and avoid the obvious pitfalls such as glutinous rice and sweet sauces you can usually find some dishes on the menu to suit. Steamed vegetables are the best area to aim for. You will find high sodium levels in many of the sauces and most restaurants use saturated and trans fat oils in cooking. There are better options for take-away so use them infrequently.

INDIAN This is probably your best choice. Indian cuisine uses a lot of fruit, vegetables, legumes and whole grains. Keep away from food that has been deep-fried, as 'ghee' (clarified and evaporated butter) is a highly saturated fat and is frequently used. Choose baked or grilled dishes and not those covered in thick sauces.

PIZZA Pizza just shouldn't be an option on your list!

What to snack on I can't stress enough how important it is to have three snacks every day. Snacks play a critical role between meals by giving you a boost when you most need it. Choose fruit; fat-free fruit yoghurt with sweetener, cottage cheese; raw vegetables or nuts. Watch out for other products that claim to be fat- and sugar-free, such as packaged puddings. Unfortunately these products are usually made with highly processed grain and are high Gi.

You might also want to look into nutrition (cereal) bars. Choose 50–65g bars that have around 200 calories each with 20–30g of carbohydrates, 12–15g of protein and 5g of fat – Tesco Healthy Living nutrition bars are a good choice. The rest are often high Gi, high calorie, and contain lots of quick-fix carbs. Check the labels carefully.

SUMMARY

Remember when eating out:

1. Bowl of bran cereal before going out.

2. Drink water on arrival – red wine later with the main course.

3. Ask for the bread basket to be taken away from the table.

4. Choose a soup or salad for the first course, preferably a vegetable/bean soup and not cream based. Ask for salad dressings to be served separately.

5. Two vegetables in lieu of potatoes/rice.

6. Poultry, veal and seafood are the best choices for the main course. Never choose fried food.

7. All sauces should be served on the side.

8. Desserts: avoid or ask for extra forks. Choose fresh fruit/berries, if available.

9. Choose decaffeinated coffee; avoid liqueurs and hot chocolate.

10. Eat slowly.

8 Your Gi questions and answers

Remember to consult your doctor prior to starting any diet or
activity plan.

Reading this book may have raised some queries and here are
some of the most common questions that we get.

**Q: Should I take vitamins and supplements when following
a lower Gi plan?**

A: Most people can get all the vitamins and minerals they need
from their diet. If, however, you feel that your diet is not balanced
or adequate for any reason, a multivitamin and mineral supplement
may be a good idea as a backstop. Vitamins and supplements
may also be appropriate for specific dietary requirements. The
Nutricentre can advise on specific vitamins and minerals that
may be appropriate. Visit www.nutricentre.com for details.

Q: Can I eat unlimited lower Gi food?

A: No. Since some lower Gi foods are high in calories and saturated fat
they should be avoided (see listings on page 118 for your best choices).
Otherwise moderation and common sense are your best guides.

**Q: What is the difference between low carb and low Gi? How does
this plan differ from some of the popular low carb diets?**

A: They are completely different. Low-carb diets involve severely
limiting your carb intake in order to focus more on fats and proteins
for your energy needs. Our plan recommends that you get 50–60%
of your energy per day from carbohydrates (which equates to 312-
375g of carbohydrates for an adult male and 250–300g for an adult
female), compared to 5–6% on some low-carb diets . Our plan is
based on eating the right carbohydrates, not limiting them.

However, some of the low-carb diets do concentrate on the use of lower Gi foods, especially in their later stages where more carbohydrates are permitted. In this very limited sense they can be seen as using some of the Gi principles.

Q: What is the problem with low carb diets?
A: There are a number of criticisms that have been raised:

• Critics of low-carb diets argue that with these diets a lot of your energy comes from protein, which is very filling. This means that you eat less overall, so really these diets become a version of a 'traditional' calorie-controlled diet, albeit an unbalanced one.

• They force the body to use fats and proteins as energy rather than glucose, the latter being the quickest way for the body to create energy. This entails running down your glucose stores within the body, which leads to tiredness and lethargy.

• The breakdown of glucose involves the release of water, which puts your body at risk of dehydration. Much of the early apparent 'weight loss' on low-carb diets is in fact water loss, not fat.

• They restrict carbohydrates, meaning that the body must obtain glucose by converting the amino acids into glucose. Even if you are eating lots of protein you will still tend to lose muscle tissue, which reduces the definition in your physique, lowers your strength and slows your metabolism, which means you burn fewer calories each day. it can be very hard to exercise on a low-carb diet.

• As this muscle loss continues, critics argue that you have to lower the amount you eat to be able to continue sustaining weight loss. This means that food cravings may become unbearable and followers will 'fall off the wagon'.

• There are no long-term studies of the effects of these diets on your health, which is a worry.

Q: How can I convert from a low-carb diet to the Gi plan?
A: You need to reintroduce your carbs gradually until you are getting 50–60% of your energy from lower-Gi carbohydrates. It would be helpful to start some low intensity exercise to increase your metabolism.

Q: Can I just follow the Gi plan without getting more active?
A: Yes, but weight loss won't be as fast as it would if you exercise. Also, you won't have the fitness gains and enjoy the 'feel good' factor that comes with it; you will miss out on the extra body definition that comes with muscle gain. This in turn will mean that you won't increase your metabolism and thus burn more calories each day.

Q: What are the guidelines for good health?
A: A balanced diet is made up of a mix of foods from the four main food groups:
• bread, other cereals and potatoes
• fruit and vegetables
• meat, fish and alternatives
• milk and dairy foods.
Foods containing fat or sugar can also be incorporated into a healthy diet, but these should be in smaller amounts.
Follow the Government's '8 guidelines for a healthy diet', as below:
• Enjoy your food.
• Eat a variety of different foods.
• Eat the right amount to be a healthy weight.
• Eat plenty of foods rich in starch and fibre.
• Eat plenty of fruit and vegetables (at least five portions a day).
• Don't eat too many foods that contain a lot of fat.
• Don't have sugary foods and drinks too often.
• If you drink alcohol, drink sensibly.

Q: What about alcohol? I like a drink every now and then?
A: Alcohol should be avoided if you hope to lose weight. If, however, you have reached your target weight, a maximum of one glass of wine with dinner is allowed. (See page 29 for more information.)

Q: How much water should I drink?
A: About 2 litres a day – this is 8–10 cups or glasses a day. One tip is to take a large bottle of water to work and aim to finish it by the end of the day. Tea, diet drinks, sugar-free squash, coffee and unsweetened juices all count towards this target. Water is an essential part of getting and staying healthy. Over half of our bodies consist of water. Water is continuously lost from our bodies during the day through urine, sweat and even in our breath. It is important to keep a check on our water (hydration) levels and replace lost fluids. Even a small reduction in hydration can have a direct impact on our long-term health – it can also reduce our concentration span and stop us exercising or playing sport as well as we would want to. Remember, thirst is a poor indicator of dehydration. Drink regularly before you feel thirsty.

Q: How much weight should I expect to lose on this plan?
A: This is variable since the rate of weight loss is closely tied to how much weight you need to lose. For further details see pages 30–31.

Q: I am doing lots of exercise but not losing any weight. Why?
A: If you are doing regular weight training or high-intensity exercise, remember that you are laying down muscle, which is heavier than fat pound for pound. So you are shaping up, not losing weight, but your body fat is reducing. Remember muscle helps to burn fat by increasing your metabolism, which speeds weight loss.

Q: How often should I weigh myself?
A: Weigh yourself, without clothes, once a week at the same time –
preferably in the morning before you eat breakfast (and after going
to the toilet). This will give a more accurate reading. Don't get
obsessive – it is the body composition that is most important, i.e. the
amount of fat you have and the way you look – your shape rather
than how much you weigh.

Q: I have 'fallen off the wagon'. How do I get back on it?
A: It is normal to experience the odd lapse in following a dietary
plan and it is all part of the process of changing from one way of
eating to another. Don't beat yourself up about it. Decide to move
on and concentrate on the future. Simply start where you left off,
with renewed confidence. (See page 46.)

Q: Is the Gi diet suitable for children?
A: Yes. A healthy diet with lower Gi foods is suitable for children from
the age of five. Many of these foods are also acceptable for younger
children; however, some foods such as nuts and nut products
shouldn't be given to children below three, and whole nuts shouldn't
be given until the age of five, because of the risk of choking. (See
pages 49–50.)

Q: Is the Gi diet just for people who want to lose weight?
A: No, it is for people who want to maintain or control their current
weight as well as for those who want to lose a few pounds – or even
for people just wanting to eat more healthily and feel better.

Q: Will the Gi diet work for vegetarians?
A: Yes. The Gi plan is all about carbohydrate-containing foods, which
are equally acceptable to vegetarians. The protein part of the meal,

such as the meat, poultry, fish or eggs can be swapped for other sources of protein, such as soya, mycoprotein (e.g. Quorn), nuts, seeds, pulses or dairy products. Some of these, such as nuts and pulses, have the added advantage of having a lower Gi themselves.

Q: Is skipping meals or snacks a problem?
A: Yes. Missing meals is not going to help you achieve a healthier and slimmer you. The effect of missing a meal is that your metabolism (rate at which your body burns up calories) is lowered. This was useful in primitive man, when the next meal wasn't guaranteed, as it meant that the body didn't burn up important fuel so quickly. In the modern, developed world however, it simply means that you are not going to lose weight as efficiently. Also remember that breakfast is the most important meal of the day as it kick-starts your metabolism and gives you energy plus important vitamins and minerals. If you don't eat breakfast, it is more difficult to make up your requirement for vitamins and minerals later in the day.

Q: What should I look for in food labels?
A: Look out for the blue 'low' and 'medium' Gi circle on the front of Tesco own-brand products and check out the website for a complete list of tested lower Gi foods. These foods have been fully tested and been found to be lower Gi. Only foods containing carbohydrate can be tested for Gi, e.g. breads, pasta, rice, ready-made meals, cereals, pulses, fruit and veg, as it is a measure of the effect of starches and sugars on the blood sugar. You won't therefore find the Gi circle on foods containing very low or no carbs, such as meat, poultry, fish, dairy products etc.

Guideline Daily Amounts (GDAs) appear on the back of many Tesco-branded products and give an indication of the contribution a serving of a product makes towards your daily recommended intake

of calories, fat and salt. For more information on label contents
see page 26.

Q: Is the Gi diet safe for pregnant women?
A: Yes, there is no reason at all why pregnant or breastfeeding
women cannot enjoy a lower Gi way of eating, although certain
food should be avoided, e.g. shellfish. Always consult your doctor.

**Q: Why does my weight fluctuate even though I'm losing pounds
over all?**
A: Fluctuations in weight on a daily basis are mainly due to the
body's water balance and are generally not an indication of how well
you are sticking to the Gi dietary plan. Ensure that you drink plenty
(see the question above on water) and your kidneys will love you for
it! As long as your weight loss is slow but sure, this is a good
indication that you are on the right lines.

Q: I seem to have hit a plateau. What should I do?
A: This is normal and, if you think about it, is to be expected as your
body has now adjusted to the decreased calorie intake. If you wish
to lose more weight, kick start it into action again by increasing the
frequency and/or duration of your activity sessions, and exercise just
that little bit more vigorously. Also try to cut down your portion size
slightly at meal times. (See page 46.)

Q: I am gluten intolerant. Can I still use the Gi diet?
A: Yes, absolutely, as long as the foods you choose are free of gluten
(found in wheat, barley, rye and oats). There are now many gluten-
free alternatives to ordinary foods on the market. Tesco stocks an
excellent range of Free From foods, and has a total of 170 different
products that are gluten and wheat free. Many of these are lower Gi.

Q: How do I remember the Gi ratings for each food?
A: Tesco is making this easy for customers by starting a programme of food labelling – so look for the blue label. You don't need to remember numbers themselves just general foods that are lower Gi, such as Basmati rice or granary bread – a few simple changes will add up to something powerful.
Information on the Tesco Gi ediet is available on www.tescodiets.com. There is also information published in store.

Q: Will I still be able to go out to restaurants?
A: Of course! Try to remember a few key foods that are lower Gi, such as granary breads, basmati rice, pasta and most fruits and vegetables. Base your meal choices around these and this will bring down the overall Gi value of the meal. If you have difficulty in finding these choices on the menu, ask the manager if they'll consider providing some in the future. Remember restaurants like to supply what their clientele demands! Here are some pointers:
• Italian – pasta, mixed salads (choose low-fat dressings such as yogurt-based ones)
• Indian – Basmati rice (check with the restaurant), noodles and dishes containing pulses such as dhal
• Chinese – avoid, but, if you do eat this type of food, choose noodles or dishes containing nuts or beans/peas
• English – pasta, noodles, small new potatoes, beans, peas, lentils, granary bread, fruit and vegetables

9 Menu plans and recipes

MENU PLANS AND RECIPES

In order to get you started, we have composed menu plans for seven days' worth of meals. We hope they will show you just how broad a variety of foods you can eat and how tasty recipes with lower Gi foods can be. The recipes are not necessarily appropriate for those concerned about weight loss or control. In many cases you can substitute some ingredients with low-fat equivalents. *Bon appetit*!

DAY 1:
Breakfast
Fruity Porridge (page 84)
Lunch
Warm Sausage, Spinach & Cannellini Bean Salad (page 87)
Packed lunch option
Nutty Banana Sandwich (page 92)
Dessert
Tesco yoghurt or fromage frais or probiotic drink or fruit smoothie (page 95)
Evening Meal
Courgette Pasta with Tarragon (page 99)
Dessert
Green Figs with Apple & Honeyed Sweet Cheese (page 108)

DAY 2:
Breakfast
Strawberries & Yoghurt (page 84)
Lunch
Spinach & Cheese Frittata (page 88)

Packed lunch option
Pesto Pitta Pockets (page 92)
Dessert
Tesco low-fat natural yoghurt
+ 1 small sliced Tesco banana
+ 15g (½ oz) sultanas (page 95)
Evening Meal
Chicken & Vegetable Stir-fry (page 104)
Dessert
Summer Heaven (page 109

DAY 3:
Breakfast
Muesli & Apple (page 84)
Lunch
Sun-dried Tomato, Pea & Pancetta Soup (page 89)
Packed lunch option
Spinach Salad with Lentils & Feta (page 92)
Dessert
Piece of Tesco fruit – choose from grapes, apple, pear, strawberries,

81

orange, pink grapefruit, peach,
kiwi, tangerine, apricot, banana,
plums, cherries (page 95)

Evening Meal
Moroccan Chicken (page 105)

Dessert
Apricot & Banana Crumble (page 111)

DAY 4:

Breakfast
Breakfast Smoothie (page 85)

Lunch
Pasta Primavera (page 90)

Packed lunch option
Turkey Wrap (page 94)

Dessert
Tesco honey-topped Greek-style
yoghurt + handful of berries
(blueberries, blackberries,
cranberries, etc.) (page 95)

Evening Meal
Coley Gratin with a Vegetable
Medley (page 103)

Dessert
Baked Apples with Apricot & Orange
Butter (page 112)

DAY 5:

Breakfast
Scrambled Eggs with Cherry
Tomatoes (page 86)

Lunch
Beanburger Pittas (page 88)

Packed lunch option
Mediterranean Cheese Sandwich
(page 93)

Dessert
½ a grapefruit with a sprinkling
of sugar + Tesco roasted,
chopped hazelnuts (page 95)

Evening Meal
Spinach & Ham Lasagne (page 100)

Dessert
Fruit Salad Layers (page 110)

DAY 6:

Breakfast
Oat Cocktail (page 86)

Lunch
Beany Jacket Potato (page 91)

Packed lunch option
Italian Flag Salad (page 93)

Dessert
2 slices Tesco value malt loaf or Finest
fruit & cinnamon bread + scraping of
low-fat spread or olive oil (page 95)

Evening Meal
Spaghetti With Tuna & Sun-Dried
Tomatoes (page 102)

Dessert
Minty Citrus Fruit Salad (page 110)

DAY 7:

Breakfast
Breakfast Sundae (page 85)
Lunch
Spinach, Couscous & Mozzarella
Mushrooms (page 90)
Packed lunch option
Fruity Rice Salad (page 94)
Dessert
½ can of Tesco pears in juice + dollop
of Tesco probiotic prune yoghurt (see
page 95)
Evening Meal
Chickpea Stew with Chorizo &
Tomatoes (page 100)
Dessert
Peach & Nutmeg Bread Pudding
(page 113)

ENTERTAINING MEAL OPTIONS

OPTION 1
Starter
Vegetable Crudités with a Quick Dip
(page 95)
Main
Chicken Breasts with Lime & Ginger
(page 106)
Dessert
Baked Bananas (page 116)

OPTION 2
Starter
Warm Lentil Salad with Onion,
Lardons & Goats' Cheese Toast
(page 96)
Main
Sesame-Topped Salmon with
Asian Noodles (page 104)
Dessert
Ginger Poached Pears (page 115)

OPTION 3
Starter
Coconut Chicken Noodle Soup
(page 97)
Main
Abbacchio alla Cacciatora (page 107)
Dessert
Peach & Raspberry Cups (page 116

OPTION 4
Starter
Warm Pepper and Avocado Salad
(page 98)
Main
Sweet Potatoes Stuffed With Bacon
& Herbs (page 101)
Dessert
Filo Tarts With Apples & Sultanas
(page 117)

BREAKFASTS

FRUITY PORRIDGE

SERVES 1

50g (1½oz) Tesco organic porridge oats
300ml (10fl oz) water or semi-skimmed milk
handful of Tesco dried, ready-to-eat apricots, chopped
handful of Tesco sultanas
honey to taste

1 Make the porridge according to the instructions on the pack.
2 Add the apricots and sultanas and sweeten with honey to taste.
alternative choice: Top with a handful of fresh Tesco blueberries.

STRAWBERRIES & YOGHURT

SERVES 1

1 x 150g pot of Tesco low-fat strawberry yoghurt
1 Tesco banana – sliced
5 Tesco strawberries – cut in half
2 slices Tesco Finest fruit and cinnamon bread spread
thinly with low-fat spread or olive oil-based margarine

1 Mix the yoghurt and fruit together.
2 Serve with the bread.

MUESLI & APPLE

SERVES 1

75g (2¾oz) Tesco Finest muesli
100–150ml (4–5fl oz) Tesco semi-skimmed milk
Tesco Cox apple
Sprinkling of cinnamon

1 Pour the milk over the muesli.
2 Slice the apple on top.
3 Sprinkle cinnamon over.

BREAKFAST SMOOTHIE

SERVES 1

1 banana
100g (3½oz) pineapple, crushed
50g (1¾oz) mango, cut into pieces
1 peach, diced
1 glass of Tesco skimmed milk

1 To save time, put everything into the blender except the banana, the night before and store in the fridge.
2 In the morning, slice the banana roughly and add to the blender.
3 Blend for 1 minute and pour into a glass.

BREAKFAST SUNDAE

SERVES 1

40g (1½oz) dried fruit, roughly chopped
2 Tesco juicing oranges
40g (1½oz) breakfast cereal, such as Tesco Strawberry Crisp
70g (2½oz) fresh fruit (e.g. chopped kiwi, mango or any kind of berries)
1 x 125g pot Tesco value low-fat peach melba yoghurt or Tesco natural low-fat yoghurt

1 Soak the dried fruit overnight in the juice (if you forget, you can microwave on high for 1 minute, then allow to cool a bit).
2 Place alternate layers of soaked dried fruit, breakfast cereal, fresh fruit and organic yoghurt in a sundae glass and serve.

OAT COCKTAIL

SERVES 4

6 tbsp Tesco organic porridge oats
100ml (3½floz) Tesco organic milk
225g (8oz) organic fruit (e.g. apple, mango and raspberry, or try a mixture
of blueberry, plum, kiwi, strawberry or papaya)
finely grated zest of 1 organic lemon
2 tbsp lemon juice
2 tbsp organic clear honey
2 tsp organic sesame seeds
1 tbsp organic chopped walnuts
150g (5½oz) organic Greek yoghurt
berries and mint to garnish

1 Soak the oats in the milk for about 15 minutes.
2 Cut the fruit into small pieces.
3 Stir into the oat mixture the lemon zest and lemon juice, honey, sesame
seeds, walnuts, yoghurt and finally the fruit.
4 Spoon the mixture into individual glasses and serve decorated with berries
and a sprig or two of fresh mint.

SCRAMBLED EGGS WITH CHERRY TOMATOES

SERVES 1

2 eggs
salt and black pepper
1 tbsp full-fat milk
a little fresh flat-leaf parsley
2 slices of Tesco Finest multigrain batch bread
25g (1oz) butter, plus more for spreading
3 cherry tomatoes
orange juice and tea, to serve

1 Crack both eggs against the side of a bowl and pull the shell apart with your
thumbs. If any bits of shell fall in, use half of the empty shell to scoop them out.
Make them tasty – add a little salt and pepper. Pour in the milk.

2 Take a pair of scissors and snip some parsley into the bowl with the eggs. Whisk everything together with a fork.

3 Pop the bread into the toaster and toast until golden. Butter the toast and put on a plate ready to serve.

4 Wash the tomatoes, then slice in half.

5 Get scrambling – melt a teaspoon of butter in a frying pan over a medium heat. Pour in the egg mixture and stir until thick, but still creamy. Add the tomatoes, then spoon onto the bagel.

6 Serve with a glass of chilled orange juice and a cup of tea.

LUNCHES

WARM SAUSAGE, SPINACH & CANNELLINI BEAN SALAD
SERVES 4
4 pork sausages
3 tbsp olive oil
2 garlic cloves, crushed
2 x 300g tins Tesco cannellini beans
1 small red onion, thinly sliced
100g (3½oz) Tesco baby spinach
zest and juice of 1 lemon
salt and black pepper

1 Preheat the grill. Place the sausages on a roasting sheet and put under the grill for 5 minutes on each side, until cooked through and golden. Cut into thick slices.

2 Meanwhile, put the olive oil and garlic in a wide saucepan and heat gently for 1 minute. Stir in the cannellini beans and sliced onion. Season with salt and freshly ground black pepper and continue to cook over a low heat for 5 minutes to soften.

3 Remove the pan from the heat and toss in the sausages, along with the spinach, and lemon zest and juice.

4 Transfer to a large salad bowl and season with salt and freshly ground black pepper.

SPINACH & CHEESE FRITTATA

SERVES 4

150g (5½oz) Tesco baby new potatoes
1 tbsp olive oil
½ small red onion, thinly sliced
½ small orange pepper, thinly sliced
100g (3½oz) baby spinach leaves
salt and freshly ground black pepper
4 large free-range eggs, beaten
50g (1¾oz) Red Leicester cheese, grated

1 If using new potatoes, halve and parboil for 5 minutes until tender.
2 Preheat grill.
3 Heat the oil in a small non-stick frying pan. Sauté the onion, pepper and potatoes for 5 minutes, add the spinach and cook for another minute until it wilts.
4 Season the beaten eggs well and pour into the pan on top of the vegetables. Add half of the cheese, stir to combine, and cook on a medium heat for about 5 minutes until the mixture has set all around the edges.
5 Sprinkle the remaining cheese over the surface and put the pan under a hot grill. Grill until puffy and golden and completely set – about 5 minutes more.

BEANBURGER PITTAS

SERVES 4

100g (3½oz) 0%-fat Greek-style yoghurt
juice of ½ a lime
70g (2½oz) mixed salad leaves, such as Finest Primavera
4 Tesco wholemeal pitta breads
For the burgers:
70g (2½oz) onion, finely chopped
1 garlic clove, crushed
1½ tbsp vegetable oil
280g (10oz) Tesco canned kidney beans, mashed
70g (2½oz) carrot, grated
50g (1¾oz) Tesco Scottish porridge oats
1 tbsp Vegemite
handful of torn basil leaves

1 First make the burgers by frying the onion and garlic in half the oil until just brown, then combine with the remaining ingredients. When cool enough to handle form into 4 burger shapes.

2 Brush the burgers with the remaining oil and grill on high for 3 minutes on each side.

3 Mix the yoghurt and lime juice.

4 Divide the salad leaves between the warmed pitta breads and pop a burger into each.

5 Top each burger with a little yoghurt and serve.

SUN-DRIED TOMATO, PEA & PANCETTA SOUP

SERVES 4

½ tbsp olive oil
½ onion, finely chopped
1 garlic clove, crushed
2 tbsp sun-dried tomato paste
1 x 600g can Tesco chopped tomatoes
1 x 130g pack cubed pancetta
600ml (1 pt) chicken stock
100g (3½oz) Tesco mini pasta bows
75g (2¾oz) Tesco frozen peas
½ x 250g pack Tesco Finest baby plum tomatoes, halved
basil leaves, to garnish
slices of Tesco Finest multigrain batch bread

1 Heat the olive oil in a large pan and fry the onion for 4–5 minutes until soft but not coloured.

2 Add the garlic clove, tomato paste and chopped tomatoes.

3 Reduce the heat and cook for 10–15 minutes.

4 Meanwhile, fry the pancetta in a non-stick frying pan for 4–5 minutes until crisp. Drain on kitchen paper.

5 Add the chicken stock to the tomato mixture, bring to the boil and add the pasta bows. Cook for 5 minutes.

6 Add the peas, tomatoes and the pancetta and cook for 2 minutes more.

7 Season to taste and garnish with basil leaves.

8 Serve with slices of bread.

PASTA PRIMAVERA

SERVES 4

1 tbsp sunflower oil

1 x 225g bag Tesco baby spinach

1 x 250g Tesco brunch asparagus, trimmed and cut into small pieces

125g (4½oz) frozen shelled broad beans, defrosted and skinned

500g (1lb 2oz) Tesco fresh peas (unshelled weight), shelled

125g (4½oz) Tesco green beans, halved

6 tbsp Tesco natural, low-fat yoghurt

1 bunch spring onions, finely sliced

1 tbsp finely chopped tarragon, plus extra to garnish

salt and freshly ground black pepper

350g (12oz) Tesco dried penne pasta

1 Heat the oil in a saucepan; add the spinach, cover and cook for 5 minutes or until the leaves wilt. Set aside to cool.

2 Cook the asparagus in a little boiling water for 3 minutes, then add the broad beans, peas and green beans and cook for 2 minutes or until tender. Drain.

3 Blend the spinach and low-fat yoghurt to a purée in a food processor or with a hand blender.

4 Return the purée to the pan and stir in the drained vegetables. Mix in the spring onion, tarragon and seasoning and keep warm over a low heat.

5 Meanwhile, cook the pasta in boiling salted water according to the packet instructions until tender but still firm to the bite. Drain, then toss with the spinach and garnish with extra tarragon.

SPINACH, COUSCOUS & MOZZARELLA MUSHROOMS

SERVES 4

8 large mushrooms, about 150g (5½oz) each

salt and freshly ground black pepper

50g (1¾oz) butter

200g (7oz) Tesco couscous

2 medium onions, sliced

2 tbsp olive oil

2 x 150g packs mozzarella cheese, diced
50g (1¾oz) grated parmesan cheese
1 x 250g bag Tesco spinach, roughly chopped
Tesco large granary baps to serve

1 Preheat the oven to 200°C/400°F/Gas Mark 6.
2 Remove and chop the stalks from the mushroms. Season and dot with butter.
3 Cook in the oven for 15–20 minutes.
4 Meanwhile, cook the couscous according to pack instructions.
5 Sauté the onions and the mushroom stalks in the olive oil until golden.
6 Mix in the mozzarella cheese, parmesan and spinach.
7 Add to the drained couscous, season and fill the mushrooms with this mixture.
8 Return to the oven for 10 minutes.
9 Serve with baps.

BEANY JACKET POTATO

SERVES 4
4 baking potatoes – cooked
green salad with Tesco cherry tomatoes to serve
2 cans of any of the following:
Tesco Hot & Spicy Mixed Beans (300g can)
Tesco Vinaigrette Mixed Beans Salad (300g can)
Tesco Mixed Beans Italienne (300g can)
Tesco Three Bean Salad (300g can)
Tesco Healthy Living Baked Beans (420g can)
Tesco Baked Beans In Tomato Sauce (420g can)
Tesco Value Baked Beans with Vegetarian Sausages in Tomato Sauce (420g can)
Tesco Mexican Style Chilli Beans (420g can)
Tesco Mixed Vegetable Chilli (400g can)
Tesco Taco Mix Beans (300g can)

1 Heat up the beans as directed on the cans, and use as a filling for the baked potatoes.
2 Serve with a crisp, green salad and Tesco cherry tomatoes.

PACKED LUNCHES

NUTTY BANANA SANDWICH

SERVES 4

8 slices Tesco multigrain batch bread
crunchy peanut butter
2 bananas, sliced
runny honey

1 Spread 4 slices of bread with peanut butter.
2 Top with sliced banana.
3 Drizzle on the runny honey to taste.
4 Place remaining 4 slices on top and cut in half.

PESTO PITTA POCKETS

SERVES 4

4 slices lean back bacon, cut in 1cm (½in) strips
8 Tesco wholemeal pitta breads
12 tbsp plain fromage frais
4 tbsp green pesto
24 black olives, pitted
2 small green peppers, chopped into 1cm (½in) squares
freshly ground black pepper

1 Grill the bacon until crisp and dab with kitchen towel to absorb excess fat.
2 Slit the pitta breads down one side to make a pocket.
3 Mix the rest of the ingredients and pile into the pitta pockets.

SPINACH SALAD WITH LENTILS & FETA

SERVES 4

2 x 300g cans Tesco green lentils, drained and rinsed
1 red pepper, deseeded and finely chopped
1 x 150g pack radishes, quartered
8 tbsp dressing, such as Tesco Finest sherry vinegar
and wholegrain mustard dressing
1 x 225g bag Tesco baby spinach

1 x 200g pack feta cheese
salt and freshly ground black pepper

1 Combine the lentils, pepper and radishes.
2 Pour over the dressing, mix well and season.
3 Just before serving, toss with the spinach and crumble over the feta.

ITALIAN FLAG SALAD

SERVES 1
5 Tesco cherry tomatoes, halved
150g (5½oz) Tesco canned cut green beans
50g (1¾oz) mozzarella cheese, cubed
5 pitted, black olives, halved
olive oil or vinaigrette dressing
freshly ground black pepper
Tesco mini white pitta breads

1 Mix the vegetables and cheese together. Toss in vinaigrette dressing or olive oil and black pepper.
2 Serve with pitta breads.

MEDITERRANEAN CHEESE SANDWICH

SERVES 1
2 slices Tesco Finest oatmeal batch bread
olive oil-based spread or low-fat spread
1 tbsp sun-dried tomato purée
25g (1oz) cheddar cheese, grated
1 Tesco medium tomato, sliced

1 Spread both sides of bread with margarine.
2 On one slice spread the sun-dried tomato paste.
3 Sprinkle on the cheese and place the slices of tomato on top, finishing with the second slice of bread.
4 Cut into 2.

TURKEY WRAP

SERVES 1
50g (1¾oz) cooked turkey, chopped
low calorie coleslaw
2 Tesco wholemeal pitta bread pockets
cranberry sauce

1 Combine the turkey with the coleslaw.
2 Spread the inside of each pitta with cranberry sauce and fill with the turkey mixture.

FRUITY RICE SALAD

SERVES 4
150g (5½oz) Tesco brown basmati rice
1 tbsp olive oil
1 medium onion, diced
½ tsp each turmeric, ground ginger and ground coriander
50g (1¾oz) Tesco Australian sultanas
75g (3½oz) seedless green grapes
40g (1½oz) toasted flaked almonds
salt and freshly ground black pepper

1 Cook the rice according to the pack instructions.
2 Heat the oil in a large frying pan and sauté the onion and celery for 3–4 minutes.
3 Stir in the spices and cooked rice, then add the fruit and flaked almonds. Season and mix well.
4 Serve the salad warm or cold.

SIMPLE PUDDINGS FOLLOWING LUNCH

- Tesco yoghurt (refer to list for low or medium Gi ones)
- Tesco fromage frais (refer to list for low or medium Gi ones)
- Tesco low-fat natural yoghurt + 1 small sliced Tesco banana + 15g (½oz sultanas)
- Tesco probiotic drink
- Piece of Tesco fruit – grapes, apple, pear, strawberries, orange, pink grapefruit, peach, kiwi, tangerine, apricot, banana, plums, cherries
- Tesco honey-topped Greek-style yoghurt + handful of berries (blueberries, blackberries, cranberries, etc.)
- ½ grapefruit with a sprinkling of sugar + Tesco roasted, chopped hazelnuts
- Tesco fruit smoothie
- 2 slices Tesco value malt loaf or Finest fruit & cinnamon bread + scraping of low-fat spread or olive oil
- ½ can of Tesco pears in juice + dollop of Tesco probiotic prune yoghurt

EVENING MEALS STARTERS

VEGETABLE CRUDITÉS WITH A QUICK DIP

SERVES 4

approx. 500g (1lb 2oz) fresh veg – peppers, celery, carrots, florets of broccoli and cauliflower, washed, trimmed and cut into dipping-size pieces
200g (7oz) cucumber, deseeded and finely chopped
2 heaped tsbp fresh mint, very finely chopped
250g (9oz) Tesco natural low-fat yoghurt
large pinch each of freshly ground black pepper and Malden salt
2 tsp extra virgin olive oil

1 Prepare the vegetables.
2 Mix the cucumber and all the remaining ingredients in a small bowl and stir well.
3 Serve the vegetables with dip.
ALTERNATIVE CHOICE: You can use fresh dill or chives in place of mint.

WARM LENTIL SALAD WITH ONION, LARDONS & GOATS' CHEESE TOAST

SERVES 4

225g (8oz) Tesco green lentils
1 bay leaf
4 tbsp extra virgin olive oil
1 x 130g pack Italian pancetta or thick bacon cut into lardons
250g (9oz) baby onions or small shallots, halved
1 garlic clove
4 pieces ciabatta, French bread or crusty white bread
1 tsp French mustard
2 tsp red or white wine vinegar
1 x 20g pack flat leaf parsley
200g (7oz) Tesco Finest French goats' cheese
salt and freshly ground black pepper

1 Rinse the lentils then place in a pan with the bay leaf and cover with cold water. Bring to the boil and boil briskly for 5 minutes. Reduce to a simmer and cook, half-covered, for another 20–25 minutes or until the lentils are fully tender.

2 Meanwhile, heat 1 tbsp oil in a frying pan and cook the pancetta or bacon until crisp. Remove to a plate keeping the oil in the pan.

3 Add the onions to the pan and cook gently until lightly browned and almost tender.

4 Add the cooked onions to the lentils and continue to cook for 10 minutes, then drain and stir in the pancetta or bacon.

5 Cut the garlic in half and rub over the bread. Then finely chop the garlic.

6 Use the remaining oil, mustard, vinegar and garlic to make a dressing, and add this to the drained lentils while they are still warm.

7 Set a few sprigs of parsley aside, chop the rest and stir into the lentils. Season.

8 Grill the bread on one side, then turn and top with the sliced cheese. Season with pepper then grill until the cheese is lightly browned.

9 Serve the lentils warm in bowls, topped with a cheese toast and garnished with parsley.

COCONUT CHICKEN NOODLE SOUP

SERVES 4

2 tbsp Thai green curry paste

250g (9oz) skinless chicken breast fillets, cut into chunks

¼ x 250g pack stir-fry rice noodles

90g (3oz) Tesco fine green beans, trimmed

50g (1¾oz) Tesco baby corn, cut on the diagonal

½ tbsp olive oil

1½ x 400ml cans reduced-fat coconut milk

600ml (1pt) chicken stock

50g (1¾oz) Tesco mangetout, halved diagonally

3 tbsp freshly chopped coriander

1 Mix the curry paste with the chicken.

2 Prepare the noodles according to pack instructions.

3 Cook the beans and baby corn in boiling water for 4–5 minutes until tender.

4 Heat the olive oil in a large pan and fry the chicken for 3–4 minutes.

5 Add the coconut milk and chicken stock and bring to the boil. Simmer for 5 minutes.

6 Add the noodles, beans, corn and mangetout and heat through.

7 Stir in the coriander and serve.

WARM PEPPER & AVOCADO SALAD

SERVES 4

1 large garlic clove, peeled and halved

1 yellow pepper, quartered and deseeded

5 tbsp olive oil or avocado oil

50g (1¾oz) Tesco pecan nuts

1 tbsp balsamic vinegar

1 tbsp freshly chopped coriander, plus extra to garnish

1 tsp Dijon mustard

1 small glass white wine – about 100ml (3½floz)

1 x 250g bag Tesco jardin salad

2 avocados

1 x 250g pack Tesco Finest baby plum tomatoes, halved

salt and freshly ground black pepper

1 Preheat the grill.

2 Place the garlic and pepper quarters, skin-side up, on a baking tray and drizzle with 1 tbsp oil. Grill until the pepper skin starts to blacken and the garlic is soft. Remove the skin from the pepper and squeeze the garlic out of its skin.

3 In a food processor, blend together the pepper, garlic, oil from the baking tray, half the pecans, the remaining oil, balsamic vinegar, coriander and mustard, gradually adding the wine. Season.

4 Warm the sauce in a saucepan.

5 Halve, stone, peel and slice the avocados.

6 Toss the salad gently with the avocado slices and tomatoes. To serve, drizzle the sauce over the salad and garnish with coriander and the remaining pecan nuts.

MAIN COURSE

COURGETTE PASTA WITH TARRAGON

PREP: 20 minutes **SERVES 4**

400g (14oz) Tesco dried pasta shapes
2 tbsp olive oil
25g (1oz) butter
500g (1lb 2oz) courgettes, cut into batons
1 tsp plain flour
8 tbsp milk
1 pack fresh tarragon, chopped
salt and freshly ground black pepper
50g (1¾oz) freshly grated parmesan cheese
tomato salad to serve

1 Cook the pasta according to pack instructions.
2 Meanwhile, heat the olive oil and butter in a large frying pan and sauté the courgettes until lightly golden.
3 Stir in the flour, milk, tarragon and seasoning to taste.
4 Bring to a simmer then stir into the drained pasta with the parmesan cheese. Check the seasoning before serving with a tomato salad.

SPINACH & HAM LASAGNE

PREP: 40 minutes **SERVES 4**

700g (1lb 9oz) frozen spinach, defrosted
salt and black pepper
pinch of nutmeg, freshly ground (optional)
400g (14oz) tomato sauce
1 x 250g pack Tesco value lasagne sheets
1 x 350g tub Tesco cheese sauce
250g (9oz) cooked ham
2 tbsp grated parmesan

1 Preheat the oven to 200°C/400°F/Gas mark 6.

2 Season the spinach with plenty of salt and freshly ground pepper and a pinch of nutmeg (if using).

3 Spread a quarter of the tomato sauce over the base of a 25 x 20cm (10 x 8in) ovenproof baking dish. Top with a slightly overlapping layer of pasta sheets. Spread with a third of the cheese sauce then use half the spinach to make an even layer. Cover with a layer of sliced ham.

4 Repeat the layers, starting again with the tomato sauce, this time ending with a layer of pasta sheets. Finally top with the last of the cheese sauce, then the ham, then tomato sauce.

5 Finish with an even scattering of parmesan and bake in the oven for 30 minutes, or until cooked through and golden. Allow to cool for 5 minutes before serving.

CHICKPEA STEW WITH CHORIZO & TOMATOES

PREP: about 5 minutes **SERVES 4**

1 tbsp olive oil
1 onion, thinly sliced
1 red pepper, quartered, deseeded and thinly sliced
200g (7oz) chorizo chopped
500g (1lb 2oz) Spanish tomatoes, skinned and chopped
2 x 400g cans Tesco chickpeas, drained and rinsed
300–450ml (½–¾pt) chicken stock or water
salt and freshly ground black pepper

freshly chopped parsley or coriander to garnish
Tesco Finest oatmeal baked bread to serve

1 Heat the olive oil in a flameproof casserole and cook the onion and pepper over a medium heat for about 5 minutes.
2 Add the chorizo and cook until slightly golden.
3 Stir in the tomatoes and cook until softened, then add the chickpeas and 300ml (½pt) of the stock or water. Cover and simmer for 20 minutes; check and add more liquid, if preferred or needed.
4 Season to taste and simmer for a further 10 minutes.
5 Garnish with herbs and serve with the bread.

SWEET POTATOES STUFFED WITH BACON & HERBS
PREP: about 1½ hours **SERVES 4**
4 Tesco sweet potatoes, weighing 300–400g (11–14oz) each
1 tbsp vegetable oil
1 x 250g pack streaky bacon, chopped
1 large onion, chopped
1 tsp dried thyme
2 tbsp freshly chopped chives
freshly ground black pepper
green salad to serve

1 Preheat the oven to 200°C/400°F/Gas mark 6.
2 Wash and dry the potatoes and score each one around the middle with a knife. Cook at the top of the oven for 50 minutes to 1 hour 10 minutes until cooked through. (You can cook sweet potatoes in the microwave – score them around the middle and cook on high for about 6 minutes each until tender.)
3 Meanwhile, heat the oil in a frying pan over a medium heat and cook the bacon and onion until the bacon is lightly golden and the onion is tender.
4 Stir in the herbs and season generously with pepper.
5 Split the potatoes in half lengthways and scoop out the centre of each one, keeping a thin layer of potato next to the skin. Roughly crush the scooped-out potato, then combine with the bacon and onion mixture. Use to fill the potato shells, then return to the oven for about 15 minutes to warm through.
6 Serve with a green salad.

ALTERNATIVE CHOICES: Even sweeter ideas for sweet potatoes include:
• Add a large dollop of cottage cheese to a baked jacket sweet potato, then top with a spoonful of chutney – one of our favourites is harissa-spiced chutney.
• Flavour softened butter with finely grated fresh ginger and finely grated lime zest and juice, then add to a baked jacket sweet potato.
• For an alternative stuffing, add orange zest, sherry and ground cinnamon or nutmeg to the scooped-out potato.
• Sweet potato chips are great with sausages, bacon chops or gammon steaks. Peel and cut sweet potatoes into 'fat chips'. Put them in a pan of boiling water, bring back to the boil and cook for 3 minutes. Drain well, then shallow-fry until golden and tender.
• Sweet potato crisps are delicious: peel and cut sweet potatoes into even, paper-thin slices. Deep fry in small batches (otherwise the oil in the pan will overflow), stirring frequently until pale golden. Drain on kitchen paper and season with salt and freshly ground black pepper.

SPAGHETTI WITH TUNA & SUN-DRIED TOMATOES

PREP: 25 minutes **SERVES 4**
75g (2¾oz) Tesco spaghetti
½ x 185g can tuna chunks in sunflower oil
1 red onion, halved and thinly sliced
1 garlic clove, chopped
6 olives, stoned and sliced
6 sun-dried tomatoes, sliced
salt and freshly ground black pepper
8 fresh basil leaves, to garnish

1 Cook the spaghetti according to the pack instructions.
2 Meanwhile, heat the oil from the can of tuna in a pan; add the onion and garlic and cook until just soft.
3 Stir in half the tuna and the remaining ingredients and warm through.
4 Drain the spaghetti, reserving a little of the cooking water.
5 Add the spaghetti and reserved liquid to the tuna mixture, toss together well. Season to taste.

6 Garnish with basil leaves and serve.

ALTERNATIVE CHOICE: You can add a few capers or a dash of fresh lemon juice for a sharper flavour if wished.

COLEY GRATIN WITH A VEGETABLE MEDLEY

SERVES 4

4 x 170g (6oz) thick coley or cod fillet, fresh or frozen

salt and pepper

4 dots of butter

4 dashes of lime or lemon juice

60g (2¼oz) cheese, grated

4–8 rashers of grilled lean back bacon, chopped

stir-fry vegetables and Tesco 'Ready to Wok' medium egg noodles to serve

1 Preheat the grill.

2 Place the fish onto a lightly greased grill pan and season.

3 Dot with the butter and sprinkle with lime or lemon juice.

4 Grill for 8–10 minutes (15–20 minutes if frozen).

5 Sprinkle with the cheese and top with bacon.

6 Return to the grill and continue to cook for a further 1–2 minutes.

7 Serve with stir-fry vegetables and noodles.

SESAME-TOPPED SALMON WITH ASIAN NOODLES

SERVES 4

4 salmon fillets

Tesco Finest sesame oil for brushing plus

2 tbsp sesame seeds

juice of 1 lime

2 tbsp light soy sauce

1 tsp clear honey

1 chilli, deseeded and chopped

½ small pack coriander, chopped

1 x 250g pack Tesco fresh noodles

1 x 100g pack Tesco asparagus

1 Preheat the grill.

2 Brush the salmon with the sesame oil and sprinkle with sesame seeds.

3 Cook under the grill for 10 minutes.

4 Meanwhile, make a dressing by mixing 2 tbsp of the sesame oil, lime juice, soy sauce, honey, chilli and coriander (reserving some for garnish).

5 Cook the noodles and asparagus tips for 3 minutes in boiling salted water. Drain.

6 Toss with the dressing and serve with the salmon fillets.

7 Garnish with the rest of the coriander and serve with extra-light soy sauce.

CHICKEN & VEGETABLE STIR-FRY

SERVES 4

1 small pepper, any colour, deseeded and cut into strips

1 small onion, peeled and sliced

1 large carrot, peeled and cut into matchsticks

100g (3½oz) baby corn, sliced

150g (5½oz) mangetout

100g (3½oz) small mushrooms, wiped and cut into quarters

4 red chillies

220g bean sprouts

250g pack Tesco Ready to Wok medium egg noodles

1 tbsp vegetable oil

200g (7oz) cooked chicken, cut into strips
1 jar or sachet of stir-fry sauce (e.g. black bean or sweet and sour)

1 Prepare the vegetables.
2 Bring a large pan of water to the boil and cook the noodles according to pack instructions.
3 Heat the oil in a large pan or wok (let it get quite hot), add the peppers and onion and stir-fry for 1 minute, stirring constantly, until they begin to soften.
4 Add the carrot and baby corn and stir-fry for 1 minute.
5 Add the rest of the vegetables and stir-fry for 1 minute.
6 Add the cooked chicken, noodles and the stir-fry sauce; bring to the boil, then turn down the hest and simmer for 3–5 minutes.

MOROCCAN CHICKEN

SERVES 4
3 tbsp vegetable oil
3 medium onions, grated or finely chopped
4 chicken quarters or 8 chicken thighs, skinned
1kg (2lb 4oz) Tesco tomatoes
¼ tsp ground ginger
2 tsp ground cinnamon
2 tbsp clear honey
2 tbsp Tesco sesame seeds, toasted
salt and freshly ground black pepper
Tesco couscous to serve

1 Heat the oil in a large pan. Add the onions and chicken and fry until lightly browned.
2 Add the tomatoes and spices, and season. Cover and cook gently, turning the chicken occasionally until the flesh is so tender that it can be pulled off the bone easily.
3 Remove the chicken and reduce the sauce to a thick sizzling 'cream'. Stir as it begins to caramelise and be careful that it does not stick or burn.
4 Add the honey and return the chicken pieces to the sauce and heat through.
5 Serve the chicken with the sauce and sprinkled with sesame seeds.
6 Accompany with Tesco couscous.

CHICKEN BREASTS WITH LIME & GINGER

PREP: about 1 hour plus 1–2 hours for marinating **SERVES 4**

4 free-range chicken breast fillets, skin on

2 cloves garlic, roughly chopped

2 tbsp roughly chopped fresh ginger

1 fresh green chilli, deseeded and roughly chopped

finely shredded zest of 1 lime

1 tsp coriander seeds, crushed

2–3 tbsp light soy sauce

2 tbsp groundnut OR sunflower oil

1 onion, finely chopped

150ml (¼pt) chicken stock

1 pack fresh coriander, stalks and leaves separated and chopped

200ml (7floz) canned coconut milk OR 25g (1oz) piece creamed coconut
dissolved in 200ml (7floz) hot water

juice of 1–2 limes

½–1 tsp light muscovado sugar

salt and freshly ground black pepper

Tesco Indian Basmati rice and some stir-fried Chinese greens or spinach to serve

1 Wash and pat dry the chicken and score the skin with a sharp knife.

2 Chop the garlic, ginger, chilli and lime zest very finely together or blend in
a coffee or spice mill.

3 Mix in the coriander seeds, 1 tbsp soy and spread all over the chicken.
Cover and leave to marinate in the fridge for at least an hour.

4 Heat the oil in a frying pan, brush the chicken clean and reserve the marinade.
Brown the chicken on both sides then place in a dish and set aside.

5 Lower the heat and cook the onion gently in the frying pan for 10 minutes
until soft.

6 Return the chicken to the pan with the stock, chopped coriander stalks and
half the leaves and seasoning. Cook gently, covered, for 12–15 minutes.

7 Add the marinade and coconut milk and cook, uncovered, for 5–6 minutes
or until the chicken is cooked through.

8 Add the juice of 1 lime and ½ tsp sugar and another 1 tbsp soy. Cook for a few
minutes then adjust the seasoning, adding more lime juice, sugar and/or soy to taste.

9 Serve scattered with the remaining chopped coriander.
10 Serve with rice and some stir-fried greens or spinach.

ABBACCHIO ALLA CACCIATORA (LAMB STEW WITH PARSLEY, BREADCRUMBS, ANCHOVIES & VINEGAR)

PREP: 15 minutes, plus overnight marinating

COOKING: About 2 hours **SERVES 4**

750g (1lb 10oz) lean boneless lamb (such as leg or chump), fat removed and cut into 5cm (2in) pieces

4 tbsp olive oil

3 tbsp dried natural breadcrumbs, from Tesco Finest multigrain batch bread

3 anchovy fillets

1–2 dried chillies, deseeded

4 garlic cloves

1 x 20g pack fresh flat leaf parsley, leaves only

3 tbsp white wine vinegar

1 tsp sea salt

Tesco new potatoes, or Tesco Indian Basmati rice to serve

1 Put the lamb pieces in an ovenproof dish (preferably earthenware), then add the olive oil and the breadcrumbs.

2 Chop together the anchovies, chillies, garlic and parsley, reserving some parsley to garnish, and add to the meat with the vinegar and sea salt. Mix, then cover and leave to marinate overnight in the fridge. Remove at least 2 hours before cooking.

3 Preheat the oven to 150°C/300°F/Gas mark 2.

4 Mix the meat and marinade thoroughly, then cover the dish and cook in the centre of the oven for about 1½ hours.

5 Skim as much fat as possible from the dish, then return to the oven, uncovered. Cook for a further 15–30 minutes until really tender. There should be very little liquid left in the dish but add a dash of water during cooking if it is becoming too dry.

6 Taste and adjust the seasoning, scatter with roughly chopped parsley.

7 Serve with new baby potatoes or Basmati rice.

DESSERTS

GREEN FIGS WITH APPLE & HONEYED SWEET CHEESE

PREP: 15 minutes **SERVES 4–6**

1 x 411g can green figs
2 Tesco dessert apples, peeled, cored and cut into thin sticks
25g (1oz) Tesco Australian sultanas
1 x 200g pack medium-fat soft cheese
150g (5½oz) Tesco Greek-style yoghurt
2 tbsp toasted flaked almonds
4 tbsp Greek honey, plus extra for drizzling

1 Combine the figs, apples and sultanas.
2 Mix together the cheese, yoghurt and honey.
3 Spoon some of the fruit and a dollop of the cheese onto each plate and sprinkle with almonds.
4 Drizzle each serving with honey, if wished.

SUMMER HEAVEN

PREP: 15 minutes plus cooling **SERVES 4**

450g (1lb) Tesco blackcurrants, washed

25g (1oz) fruit sugar (fructose)

300g (10½oz) Tesco 8%-fat natural fromage frais

2 tbsp Tesco skimmed milk

2 tsp icing sugar

1 ready-made individual meringue nest

4 sprigs redcurrants or blackcurrants to decorate

1 Using a fork drawn along the stalks, remove the blackcurrants. Place in a saucepan with 2 tbsp water and, over a medium heat, bring to simmering point. Turn the heat down and simmer for 3 minutes or until the blackcurrants start to burst and you have plenty of deep purple juice.

2 Add the fructose, stir to dissolve, then set aside to cool.

3 In a bowl, beat together the fromage frais, milk and sugar.

4 Put the meringue inside a plastic food bag or between two pieces of foil and crumble roughly, using a rolling pin or similar.

5 Prepare the servings: divide half the blackcurrant compôte between four wide dessert glasses. Then spoon one quarter of the fromage frais mixture into each glass, smoothing down evenly. Top with the remaining compote and finish with the meringue pieces.

6 Serve decorated with berries or chill until needed, then decorate.

FRUIT SALAD LAYERS

PREP: 10 minutes, plus 1 hour cooling **SERVES 4**

1 large Tesco red-skinned eating apple
pinch of ground cinnamon
300g (10½oz) Tesco fresh green seedless grapes, halved
125g (4½oz) Tesco fresh or frozen and defrosted raspberries, sprinkled with 2 tsp icing sugar
50g (1¾oz) Tesco fresh blueberries
300g (10½oz) Tesco natural Healthy Living bio yoghurt

1 Core and chop the apple into bite-sized pieces and sprinkle the cinnamon over the top. Leave for 1 hour in the fridge.
2 Divide the apple and grapes between four dessert glasses. Top each with one-eighth of the yoghurt. Sprinkle over the raspberries, then spoon over the remaining yoghurt. Top with the blueberries.

MINTY CITRUS FRUIT SALAD

PREP: 15–20 minutes plus chilling **SERVES 4**

2 Tesco pomelos
1 Tesco pink or ruby grapefruit
1 Tesco yellow grapefruit
3 Tesco large oranges
handful fresh mint leaves
ground cinnamon to dust (optional)

1 Holding each fruit over a large bowl, remove the peel and pith using a sharp serrated knife, then separate into segments, discarding the membrane and reserving the juices.
2 Arrange the fruit in a wide shallow serving bowl or platter, then scatter the mint leaves over the fruit.
3 Pour over the reserved fruit juices and dust very lightly with cinnamon, if using. Cover the bowl and chill for 20–30 minutes.

APRICOT & BANANA CRUMBLE

PREP: 35 minutes plus cooling **COOKING:** 25 minutes **SERVES 4**

200g (7oz) Tesco Finest ready-to-eat dried apricots

2 medium bananas

4 tbsp lemon juice

25g (1oz) Tesco chopped mixed nuts

1 tbsp Tesco sunflower seeds

75g (2¾oz) Tesco value porridge oats

1 tbsp golden syrup

25g (1oz) butter

1 tbsp dark brown sugar

fromage frais, Greek yoghurt or custard to serve

1 Preheat the oven to 190°C/375°F/Gas mark 5.

2 Simmer the apricots in a covered saucepan, with just enough water to cover, for 30 minutes or until they are very tender and plump.

3 Meanwhile, peel and slice the bananas and put into a 900ml (1½pt) baking dish. Spoon over the lemon juice and apricots with 4 tbsp of their cooking liquid.

4 In a bowl, mix together the nuts, seeds and oats.

5 Melt the syrup, butter and sugar in a saucepan and stir into the oat mixture. Spoon over the fruit and bake for 25 minutes or until golden.

6 Serve warm or cold with fromage frais, Greek yoghurt or custard.

BAKED APPLES WITH APRICOT & ORANGE BUTTER

PREP: 15 minutes **COOKING:** up to 1 hour **SERVES 4**

finely grated zest and juice of 1 Tesco jaffa orange
25g (1oz) butter, softened
50g (1¾oz) light brown soft sugar
16 Tesco Finest ready-to-eat dried apricots, quartered
4 Tesco eating apples, such as Cox's
cream, ice-cream or custard to serve

1 Preheat the oven to 180°C/350°F/Gas mark 4.
2 Beat together the orange zest, butter and sugar, then mix in the apricots.
3 Core and cut a thin slice from the top and bottom of each apple. Set in a baking dish and stuff with the apricot mixture, piling any extra on top. Spoon the orange juice and 4 tbsp water around; cover with foil.
4 Cook for about 40 minutes. They should be tender when tested with a skewer. If necessary, return to the oven, adding a little extra water, if needed, and cook for a further 15–20 minutes.
5 Serve with a little cream, ice-cream or custard.

PEACH & NUTMEG BREAD PUDDING

It's always difficult to make a pud that's low in fat and full of flavour but this one rises to the challenge!

PREP: 20 minutes, plus up to 30 minutes soaking

COOKING: 30 minutes **SERVES 4**

125g (4½oz) Tesco multigrain batch bread, cubed (no need to remove crusts)
1 x 410g can Tesco peach slices in grape juice, peaches cubed and juice reserved
150ml (¼pt) Tesco half-fat milk
1 large egg
25g (1oz) dried mixed fruit
1 tsp ground nutmeg
4 tsp demerara sugar
4 tsp butter
Tesco low-fat natural yoghurt to serve

1 Preheat the oven to 180°C/350°F/Gas mark 4.

2 Set four individual gratin dishes on a baking tray, then divide the bread and peaches between them.

3 Whisk the reserved grape juice with the milk and egg and stir in the dried fruit. Pour over the bread and leave to soak for up to 30 minutes.

4 Mix together the nutmeg and sugar and sprinkle over, then dot with the butter. Cook at the top of the oven for 30 minutes or until golden and slightly crunchy.

5 Serve with a little yoghurt, if wished.

TORTA DI RICOTTA (RICOTTA CAKE)

PREP: about 30 minutes **COOKING:** about 1 hour **SERVES** 8

75g (2¾oz) unsalted butter at room temperature, plus a little for greasing

125g (4½oz) caster sugar

2 eggs, beaten

finely grated rind and juice of ½ unwaxed lemon

finely grated rind and juice of ½ large orange

2 tbsp finely chopped cut mixed peel

3 tbsp plain flour

½ tsp baking powder

pinch of salt

2 x 250g tubs Italian ricotta, well drained

icing sugar to dust

pouring cream or orange salad to serve (optional)

1 Preheat the oven to 180°C/350°F/Gas mark 4.

2 Butter and line the base of a 20.5cm (8in) spring-release tin with baking paper. Butter the paper as well.

3 In a large bowl, beat the butter and sugar until pale and creamy.

4 Add the beaten eggs, little by little, beating thoroughly between each addition, then mix in the citrus rind and juice and the mixed peel.

5 Sift the flour, baking powder and a pinch of salt and fold into the cake mix.

6 Press the ricotta through a sieve directly into the cake-mix bowl. (This will help to aerate it.) Fold in carefully. Transfer the mixture to the tin and level the surface.

7 Cook the cake in the centre of the oven for about 1 hour until it is lightly golden and just firm to the touch (it will shrink away from the sides of the tin slightly).

8 Leave to cool in the tin, then carefully turn it out onto a plate.

9 Sprinkle with icing sugar just before serving.

10 Serve with pouring cream or an orange salad if preferred.

GINGER POACHED PEARS

You can make these in the morning, or even the night before and keep them covered in the fridge. Take them out a couple of hours before serving so the syrup becomes a little runny again.

SERVES 4

4 firm Tesco pears
5cm (2in) piece fresh ginger, peeled and thinly sliced
2 cinnamon sticks
50g (1¾oz) caster sugar
600ml (1pt) red wine
vanilla ice cream to serve

1 Peel each pear, leaving the stalk intact. Cut a thin slice off the base of each one so that they stand upright.
2 Place the pears on their sides in a large saucepan and add the ginger, cinnamon sticks, sugar and red wine
3 Bring to the boil, then cover and simmer for 30–45 minutes, turning frequently, until the pears are tender.
4 Strain the liquid through a sieve into a wide, shallow pan, then bubble over a high heat for 5–10 minutes until syrupy. (You can remove the cinnamon and ginger or leave them in for a stronger flavour.)
5 When ready to serve, place each pear in the centre of a plate, spoon around 2 tbsp syrup and serve at room temperature with vanilla ice cream.

BAKED BANANAS

PREP: 10 minutes **COOKING:** 10-15 minutes **SERVES 4**

4 Tesco clementines
2 tbsp Tesco Finest ginger preserve
8 cardamom pods, split
4 Tesco bananas
Tesco fromage frais OR Tesco natural yoghurt OR ice cream OR whipped cream to serve

1 Preheat the oven to 200°C/400°F/Gas mark 6.
2 Pare the zest from 2 clementines and squeeze the juice from all 4.
Place the zest and juice in an ovenproof dish with the ginger preserve and cardamom pods.
3 Peel and halve the bananas lengthways, then widthways. Toss them in the juice, cover and cook at the top of the oven for 10–15 minutes until just tender.
4 Serve at once with a dollop of your choice of topping.

PEACH & RASPBERRY CUPS

SERVES 4

4 Tesco peaches/nectarines
250g (9oz) Tesco raspberries
425g (14¾oz) fresh ricotta
2½ tbsp single cream
1½ tbsp clear honey
1 vanilla pod

1 Halve the peaches/nectarines and take out the stones. Place on a large platter and scatter over the raspberries.
2 Place the ricotta, cream and honey in a bowl and scrape in the seeds from 1 vanilla pod.
3 Using a balloon whisk, whisk well until the mixture is light and fluffy.
4 Serve with the fruit.

FILO TARTS WITH APPLES & SULTANAS

PREP: 10 minutes **COOKING:** 10 minutes **SERVES 4**

4 sheets Jus-Rol filo pastry
4 sprays of Tesco spray oil
25g (1oz) butter
2 apples (e.g. Tesco Granny Smith), peeled, cored and sliced
50g (1¾oz) brown sugar
50g (1¾oz) Tesco sultanas
25ml (1floz) Calvados
icing sugar to dust
2 heaped tbsp crème fraîche to serve

1 Preheat oven to 200°C/400°F/Gas mark 6.
2 Spray one sheet of pastry with oil spray and drop it, spray-side up, onto a baking tray to form a rough nest shape. Repeat with the other sheets. Bake for 8 minutes.
3 Melt the butter in a frying pan; add apples, sugar, raisins and Calvados and cook until the juices are reduced and the fruit begins to brown – about 5–10 minutes.
4 To serve, pile the apple filling into the pastry nests and sift on a little icing sugar.
5 Serve warm with the crème fraîche.

G.I. Food Listings

In the following pages you will find lists of product ranges available in Tesco. The foods have been divided into three groups – high Gi (red), medium Gi (yellow) and low Gi (green) – but since the Gi bases its measurements on the carbohydrate content in a food, it is sometimes difficult for those who want to try and lose weight to determine which foods that are officially low Gi are also good for dieting. So, any item in bold is also recommended for eating if you want to lose weight.

However, in addition, you will need to limit the portions you eat of some of those foods quite strictly. For example, nuts are shown as being a good diet food, but that doesn't mean you should overindulge. In these cases we have indicated foods that you should eat on a restricted basis with an asterisk (*).

Some of the foods listed cannot be Gi tested by standard methods as they contain no or virtually no carbohydrate. However, for the purpose of including a complete balance of foods, they have been included in the listings and are marked with a cross (†).

Foods highlighted in bold in the green channel are especially useful for weight loss.

Gi
Glycaemic Index tested

Look out for this symbol in Tesco stores.

FRESH VEGETABLES
Broad beans (500g)
Broad beans (canned, 300g)

FRESH VEGETABLES
Yams

FRESH VEGETABLES
Alfalfa sprouts
Asparagus
Aubergine
Beans (green/runner)
Bok choy
Broccoli
Brussels sprouts
Cabbage
Capers
Carrots
Cauliflower
Celery
Collard Greens
Courgettes
Cucumber
Garden peas (class 2, 500g pack)
Garden peas (loose, locally grown)
Garden peas (loose, class 2)
Garden peas (Tesco shelled, 190g pack)
Lettuce
Mangetout
Mushrooms
Mustard greens
Okra
Olives*
Onions
Parsley
Peppers
Peppers (chillis)
Pickles
Radicchio
Radishes
Sauerkraut

FRESH VEGETABLES (CONT)

Scallions
Spinach
Swiss Chard
Sugarsnap peas (160g pack)
Sugarsnap peas (300g pack)
Tomatoes
Yams (loose, class 1)

FROZEN VEGETABLES

Corn on the cob
(Birds Eye baby, 480g pack)
Corn on the cob (Tesco 4.794g pack)
Corn on the cob (Tesco mini, 907g pack)
Garden peas
(Aunt Bessie's minted, 500g pack)
Garden peas (Birds Eye, 1.82kg pack)
Garden peas (Birds Eye, 454g pack)
Garden peas (Birds Eye, 907g pack)
Garden peas (Tesco, 1.81kg pack)
Garden peas (Tesco, 907g pack)
Garden peas (Tesco minted, 907g pack)
Garden peas (Tesco organic, 907g pack)
Peas (Tesco Value, 1.81kg pack)
Peas (Tesco Value, 454g pack)
Petits pois
(Birds Eye steam-fresh, 480g pack)
Petits pois (Birds Eye, 1.36kg pack)
Petits pois (Birds Eye, 680g pack)
Petits pois (Tesco, 907g pack)
Sweetcorn (Tesco, 907g pack)
Sweetcorn (Tesco organic, 907g pack)
Sweetcorn
(Tesco Supersweet, 907g pack)
Sweetcorn (Tesco Value, 907g pack)

FROZEN VEGETABLES
Baby broad beans (750g)

FRESH FRUIT – APPLES/PEARS/CITRUS

APPLES

Braeburn (class 1, loose)
Cooking (class 1, loose)
Cooking (Tesco Value, pack)
Cox (class 1, loose)
Cox apples (class 1, 9 pack)
Empire (class 1, loose)
Gala (class 1, loose)
Gala (pack)
Gala (Tesco organic, 4 pack)
Golden Delicious (class 1)
Golden Delicious (class 1, 7 pack polybag)
Golden Delicious (class 1, loose)
Granny Smith (class 1, loose)
Granny Smith (class 1, 7 pack polybag)
Tesco Value apple bag
Tesco kids fun size apples (10 pack)

PEARS

Comice (class 1, loose)
Conference pears (class 1, loose)
Conference pears (pack)
Packham Triumph (class 1, loose)
Tesco Value pack

CITRUS

Kids easy peeler citrus pack
Lemons
Limes

CITRUS – CLEMENTINES

Clementines (800g pack)
Clementines (class 1, loose)
Clementines (Tesco Finest 4 pack)

FRUITS-FRESH

Apricots (loose)
Apricots (punnet, 500g pack)
Bananas
Kiwi
Mangos
Papaya
Pineapple

FRUITS-FRESH

Cantaloupe
Honeydew Melon
Raisins
Finest watermelon
Funsize watermelon
Lipstick watermelon
Watermelon.chunk (2x1kg)

CITRUS — GRAPEFRUIT

Grapefruit (Jaffa, 3 pack)
Grapefruit (juicing, 2kg)
Grapefruit (pink, class 1, loose)
Grapefruit (red, class 1, loose)
Grapefruit (Sweetie, class 1, loose)
Grapefruit (Tesco Value 500g)
Grapefruit (yellow, class 1, loose)

CITRUS — MANDARINS

Mandarins (800g pack)
Mandarins (class 1, loose)
Mandarins (Tesco 1.5kg pack)

CITRUS — ORANGES

Oranges (6 pack)
Oranges (class 1, loose)
Oranges (Jaffa class 1, loose)
Oranges
(Jaffa easy peeler pack, 800g pack)
Oranges (Jaffa pack)
Oranges, juicing (2.5kg pack)
Oranges (Loose)
Oranges
(Navel/Valencia large, 5 per pack)
Oranges (Tesco Finest pack)
Oranges (Tesco Value 4 pack)

CITRUS — SATSUMAS

Satsumas (800g pack)
Satsumas (1kg pack)
Satsumas (1.4kg pack)
Satsumas (class 1, loose)

FRESH FRUIT – GRAPES/STONED

Grapes
Grapes, red seedless (class 1, loose)
Grapes, seedless (class 1, pack)
Grapes, white seedless (class 1, loose)

STONED

Cherries (300g pack)
Cherries (class 1, loose bagged)
Cherries (Tesco 300g pack)
Cherries (Tesco Finest 300g pack)
Nectarines
Peaches
Plums (500 g punnet)
Plums (British, class 1, 400g punnet)
Plums (class 1, loose)
Plums (class 1, punnet)
Plums (eat me-keep me punnet)

BERRIES

Blackberries
Bluberries
Raspberries
Strawberries

OTHER

Avocado* (limit to ¼)
Guavas
Plantain (loose, class 1)
Rhubarb

ORGANIC FRESH FRUIT & VEGETABLES

Broad beans (500g)

FRUITS – BOTTLED, TINNED, FROZEN, DRIED

Apple puree containing sugar
Most dried fruit
Regular fruit spreads
Tinned Fruit in Syrup

ORGANIC FRESH FRUIT & VEGETABLES

Apricots (300g pack)

FRUITS – BOTTLED, TINNED, FROZEN, DRIED

Australian sultanas (500g)
Australian sultanas (1kg)
Dried Apples
Dried Cranberries
Extra fruit/low-sugar spreads
Fruit Cocktail in juice
Peaches/pears in syrup
Prunes
Sultanas (500g)
Sultanas (1kg)
Tesco Value sultanas (500g)
Tesco Finest pineapple slices (200g)
Tesco Fresh pineapple chunks (400g)
Tesco Ready To Eat golden pineapple (200g)

ORGANIC FRESH FRUIT & VEGETABLES

Apples (Tesco dessert tray pack)
Apples (Tesco Kids fun size)
Apples (Tesco, loose)
Apples (Tesco polybag)
Apples (Tesco red apple bag)
Clementines (800g pack)
Grapefruit (pink, twinpack)
Grapes (loose)
Grapes (Tesco red, 400g pack)
Oranges (1.5kg pack)
Oranges (4 pack)
Pears (Tesco 1kg pack)
Pears (Tesco 4 pack)
Plums (Tesco 500g punnet)
Sugarsnap peas (Tesco 200g pack)

FRUIT – BOTTLED, TINNED, FROZEN, DRIED

Apple sauce (no sugar) – eg Clearspring
Organic Apple Purée
Frozen berries
Mandarin Oranges
Peaches in juice or water
Pears in juice or water

PASTA

All tinned pasta
Gnocchi
Linguine
Macaroni and cheese
Noodles (tinned)

PASTA AND NOODLES (DRIED)

Capellini
Cellophane noodles (mung bean)
Cellentani pasta
(Buitoni Express 500g pack)
Conchiglie pasta shells (Tesco 500g pack)
Conchiglie pasta shells (Tesco 1kg pack)
Conchiglie pasta shells
(Tesco BPBV 2kg pack)
Conchiglie pasta shells – quick cook
(Tesco 1kg pack)
Creste (Tesco 500g pack)
Egg lasagne (375g pack)
Egg lasagne (Tesco 375g pack)
Egg lasagne verdi (375g pack)
Egg lasagne verdi (Tesco 375g pack)
Egg tagliatelle (500g pack)
Egg spaghetti (Tesco 500g pack)
Egg tagliatelle (Tesco 500g pack)
Eliche pasta (Buitoni 500g pack)
Farfalle pasta (Buitoni 500g pack)

Fettuccine
Fusilli pasta twists (500g pack)
Fusilli pasta twists (1kg pack)
Fusilli pasta twists (2kg pack)
Fusilli pasta twists (5kg pack)
Fusilli pasta twists (Tesco BPBV 2kg pack)
Fusilli pasta twists– quick cook
(Tesco 1kg pack)
Fusilli pasta twists – tricolore (500g pack)
Fusilli pasta twists – wholewheat
(500g pack)
Lasagne (Buitoni 250g pack)
Lasagne (Tesco 250g pack)

Lasagne (Tesco 500g pack)
Lasagne sheets (Tesco 250g pack)
Lasagne sheets (Tesco Value 250g pack)
Linguine (De cecco 500g pack)
Linguine (Tesco 500g pack)
Lumache pasta (Tesco 500g pack)
Macaroni (Tesco 500g pack)
Noodles
(frozen, express Chinese Oriental, 350g)
Penne pasta quills (Tesco 500g pack)
Penne pasta quills (Tesco 1kg pack)
Penne pasta quills
(Tesco Value 500g pack)
Penne pasta quills – quick cook
(Tesco 1kg pack)
Penne rigate pasta quills
(Buitoni 500g pack)
Penne rigate pasta quills
(Buitoni 1kg pack)
Radiatore (Tesco 500g pack)
Rigatoni

Spaghetti (Buitoni 1kg pack)
Spaghetti (Marshalls 500g pack)
Spaghetti (Tesco BPBV 2kg pack)
Spaghetti (Tesco Value 500g pack)
Spaghetti (Barilla 500g pack)
Spaghetti – long (Buitoni 500g pack)
Spaghetti – natural corn
(Orgran gourmet 250g)
Spaghetti – quick cook
(Buitoni 500g pack)
Spaghetti – quick cook (Tesco 1kg pack)
Spaghetti – short (Buitoni 500g pack)
Spaghetti – short (Tesco 500g pack)

STUFFINGS

Manor born sage & onion stuffing
(454g)
Sage & onion stuffing mix (170g)
Sage & onion stuffing mix (340g)
Sage & onion stuffing mix (85g)
Tesco Finest herb stuffing mix (115g)
Tesco Finest pork, chestnut & onion
stuffing (450g)
Tesco Finest pork, ham & leek
stuffing (440g)
Tesco Finest pork, sage and onion
stuffing

BAGELS

5 Original bagels
Organic bagels (5-pack)
Plain bagels (5-pack)
Single plain bagels
Single sundried tomato bagels
Tesco Finest bagels (twin pack)
Tesco Finest brunch bagels
(4-pack)

POTATOES

Anglesey new potatoes (loose)
Baby new potatoes (punnet, 750g)
Charlotte potatoes (750g pack)
Finest new baby red potatoes (750g pack)
Jersey new potatoes (canned, 300g)
Jersey new potatoes (canned, 538g)
Jersey Royal new potatoes (punnet, 500g)
Kentish new potatoes (1.5kg)
New potatoes (1.5kg)
New potatoes (2.5kg)
New potatoes (loose)
New potatoes (canned, 567g)
New potatoes (canned, 800g)
Organic baby new potatoes (500g pack)
Organic new potatoes (1.5kg pack)
Organic sweet potatoes (750g pack)
Scottish new potatoes (1.5kg)
Scottish new potatoes (2.5kg)
Sweet potatoes (750g pack)
Sweet potatoes (loose)
Tesco Value new potatoes (canned, 567g)
Unpeeled new potatoes (canned, 567g)
Welsh new potatoes (loose)
Welsh new potatoes (1.5kg)
Welsh new potatoes (2.5kg)

PASTA AND NOODLES (DRIED) (CONT)

Spaghetti – short (Tesco 1kg pack)
Spaghetti – wholewheat
(Tesco 500g pack)
Tagliatelle (Tesco 500g pack)
Vermicelli

FRESH PASTA

Egg fusilli – fresh
(Exp Tesco 250g pack)
Egg penne – fresh
(Exp Tesco 500g pack)
Egg penne – fresh
(Tesco 500g pack)
Egg spaghetti – fresh
(Tesco 250g pack)
Egg spaghetti – fresh
(Tesco 500g pack)
Egg spirals/fusilli – fresh
(Tesco 250g pack)
Egg tagliatelle – fresh
(Exp Tesco 250g pack)
Egg tagliatelle – fresh
(Exp Tesco 500g pack)
Egg tagliatelle – fresh
(Tesco 250g pack)
Egg tagliatelle – fresh
(Tesco 500g pack)

BREADS

Bakers Premier Gold thick sliced
white bread (800g)
Crispbreads
Croissants
Crusty white bloomer (800g)
Crusty white sliced (800g)
Doughnuts:
Iced ring confectionery
doughnuts (4-pack)
iced ring doughnuts (4-pack)
Jam doughnuts (5-pack)
Jam doughnuts (10-pack)
Jumbo jam doughnuts
Large rind doughnut (5-pack)
Mini doughnut rings (20-pack)
Mini jam dougnuts (8-pack)
Mini jammie bite doughnuts
(15-pack)
Single jam doughnuts
French bread baguette (400g)
French bread cobs (2-pack)
French bread floured batard
French bread grand rustique
French bread ploughman's rolls
(2-pack)
Hamburger buns
Healthy Living white loaf medium
sliced (400g)
Homebake half baguettes
(2-pack)
Homebake mini petit pains
(6-pack)
Hot dog buns

BREADS

10 Mini white pitta bread (180g)
Brown Multi Grain loaf (400g)
Crispbread with fibre
Finest multigrain batch bread (800g)
Finest oatmeal batch bread (800g)
Organic malt loaf (225g)
Sliced fruit loaf (400g)
Value white pitta bread (6 pack)
White Multi Grain loaf (400g)
Wholegrain breads
Wholemeal pitta bread (6 pack)

RICE

Indian Basmati rice (500g)
Indian Basmati rice (1kg)
Indian Basmati rice (2kg)
Indian Easy Cook Basmati rice (1kg)
Organic Basmati rice (500g)

NUTS AND DRIED FRUIT

Value dried, mixed fruit (500g)*

BREADS

100% stone-ground wholemeal*
Crispbreads (high-fibre)*
Finest crusty malted wheat loaf (800g)
Wholegrain, high-fibre breads*

RICE

Value Basmati rice (250g)
Value Basmati rice (1kg)

NUTS AND DRIED FRUIT

Almonds* (see page 38)
Apricots for kids (Tesco 50g pack)
Cashew nut kernels (300g)*
Cashew nuts (100g)*
Cashew nuts (Tesco 150g pack)*
(see page 38)
Cashew nuts (Tesco Value 300g pack)*
Dried pitted prunes (250g)
Hazelnuts* (see page 38)
Macadamia nuts* (see page 38)
Mixed nuts & raisins (1kg)*
Monkey nuts (Tesco Value 500g pack)*
Monkey nuts – roasted (Tesco 250g pack)*
Organic roasted, salted cashew nuts (100g)*
Pistachio nuts* (see page 38)
Ready to eat apricots (250g)

BREADS (CONT)
Kaiser rolls
Mega Value 24 white rolls
Mini white pitta bread (10-pack)
Muffins
Organic white (400g)
Organic white (800g)
Pancakes
Part-baked petits pains (12-pack)
Pikelets (8-pack)
Pizza
Premium white extra thick (800g)
Premium white medium (800g)
Round crusty rolls (4-pack)
Round crusty rolls (6-pack)
Scottish plain white sliced (800g)
Single French country roll
Single white continental
morning rolls
Single white crusty round rolls
Stayfresh white medium (800g)
Stayfresh white thick (800g)
Tesco Finest country loaf
Tesco Finest crusty white (800g)
Tesco Finest French baguette
(400g)
Tesco Finest French bread baton
Tesco Finest French bread ficelle
Tesco Finest French bread
Parisienne
Tesco Finest French bread
petit pains (4-pack)
Tesco Finest French cob
Tesco Finest French country loaf
(400g)

CEREAL GRAINS
Amaranth
Croutons
Millet
Quinoa
Rice (short-grain, white, instant)
Rice cakes

NUTS AND DRIED FRUIT (CONT)
Ready to eat apricots (500g)
Ready to eat bite size apricots (500g)
Roast, salted cashews (100g)*
Roast, salted cashews (200g)*
Roast, salted cashews (325g)*
Roast, salted cashews (400g)*
Roast, salted cashews (600g)*
Roasted salted mixed nuts (425g)*
Tesco Dried apricots (250g)
Tesco ready to eat pears (250g)

CEREAL GRAINS
Barley
Buckwheat
Bulgar
Grain flour
Kasha (toasted buckwheat)
Soya Protein Powder
Wheat berries
Wheatgrain

Tesco Finest French Couronne bread (400g)
Tesco Finest fruit & cinnamon bread
Tesco Value 12 white rolls
Tesco Value malt loaf (200g)
Tesco Value rolls, thick sliced (360g)
Tesco Value white medium sliced (800g)
Tesco Value white pitta bread (6 pack)
Tesco Value white thick sliced (800g)
Tortillas
Waffles
Potato waffles (18-pack, 1kg)
Potato waffles (8-pack, 454g)
White Continental morning rolls (4-pack)
White Danish medium sliced (400g)
White Danish thick sliced (400g)
White loaf medium sliced (800g)
White loaf thick sliced (800g)
White sliced sandwich (800g)

BEANS & PULSES (DRIED)

Butter beans (500g pack)
Haricot/navy
Italian
Lima
Mung
Pearl barley (500g pack)
Pinto
Pigeon
Red kidney beans (500g pack)
Red split lentils (500g pack)
Romano
Soy
Yellow split peas (500g pack)

TINNED

Baked beans
Baked beans in tomato sauce (420g)
Black eye beans (Tesco 300g)
Butter beans (Tesco 220g)
Butter beans (Tesco 420g)
Cannellini beans (Tesco 300g)
Chick peas (Tesco 400g)
Chick peas in salt water (Tesco 220g)
Green lentils (Tesco 300g)
Mixed salad beans
Petits pois & baby carrots (200g)
Red kidney beans (Tesco 220g)
Red kidney beans (Tesco 420g)
Red kidney beans (Tesco 3x420g pack)
Red kidney beans (Tesco Value 400g)
Red kidney beans – no added sugar or salt (Tesco 220g)
Red kidney beans – no added sugar or salt (Tesco 420g)

BEANS
Broad
Refried beans

CEREALS
Cornflakes (250g)
Cornflakes (500g)
Cornflakes (750g)
Cornflakes (1kg)
Cornflakes (organic, 500g)
Frosted flakes (500g)
Frosted flakes (750g)
Frosted flakes (1kg)
Healthy Living muesli (500g)
Healthy Living Sultana Bran (500g)
Healthy Living Sultana Bran (750g)
Honey & Nut cornflakes (500g)
Honey & Nut cornflakes (750g)
Tesco Value cornflakes (500g)
Tesco Value frosted flakes (500g)

CEREALS
Fruit muesli (500g)
Fruit muesli (1kg)
Fruit & Fibre breakfast cereal (500g)
Fruit & Fibre breakfast cereal (750g)
Fruit & Nut muesli (500g)
Organic Porridge oats (750g)
Scottish Porridge Oats (500g)
Scottish Porridge Oats (1kg)
Tesco Value Fruit & Fibre (500g)
Tesco Value muesli (1kg)
Tesco Value Porridge Oats (1kg)
Wholewheat muesli (750g)
Wholewheat muesli (1.5kg)

TINNED (CONT)
Sweetcorn (200g)
Sweetcorn (325g)
Sweetcorn (3x200g)

CEREALS
Healthy living branflakes (500g)
Healthy living branflakes (750g)
Healthy living branflakes (1kg)
Hi fibre bran breakfast cereal (750g)
Oat Bran
Porridge Oats
Soya Protein Power

MEAT, POULTRY, FISH, EGGS AND SOY†

Hamburgers
Hot dogs
Minced beef (more than 10% fat)
Pâté
Processed meats
Regular bacon
Sausages
Sushi (rice based)
Whole regular eggs

READY MEALS

Cottage pie (chilled, 500g)
Cumberland pie (chilled, 500g)
Sausage & mash (chilled, 500g)
Shepherds pie (chilled, 500g)

MEAT, POULTRY, FISH, EGGS AND SOY†

Chicken/turkey leg
Lamb (Tenderloin, Centre loin chop,
Boiled ham)
Minced beef (lean)
Pork (Fore shank, Leg shank, Centre cut,
Loin chop)
Sirloin tip
Sirloin steak
Turkey bacon
Whole omega-3 eggs

MEAT, POULTRY, FISH, EGGS AND SOY†

All seafood, fresh, frozen or tinned
(avoid breaded or battered)
Back bacon
Beef (top round steak, Eye round steak)
Chicken Breast (skinless)
Egg whites
Lean deli ham
Minced beef (extra lean)
Pork tenderloin
Quorn
Rabbit
Sashimi
Soy/whey powder
Tofu
Turkey breast (skinless), leg
Veal (cutlet, rib roast, blade steak)

READY MEALS

Beef lasagne (frozen, 400g)
Beef lasagne (frozen, 900g)
Cumberland fish bake (chilled, 1kg)
Healthy Living chicken korma & rice
(chilled, 450g)
Healthy Living chicken tikka masala/rice
(chilled, 420g)
Healthy Living meat lasagne (chilled, 340g)
Healthy Living meat lasagne (chilled, 800g)
Lasagne (chilled, 400g)
Lasagne (chilled, 950g)
Serves 1 Chicken chow mein (chilled, 475g)
Serves 1 Sweet & sour chicken with
noodles (chilled, 475g)
Spinach & ricotta cannelloni (chilled, 800g)

BISCUITS

50% reduced fat cream crackers (200g)
Cream crackers (300g)
Dutch crispbakes (100g)
Dutch melba toast (200g)
French toast (200g)
Nice biscuits (200g)
Nice biscuits (400g)
Original mini breadsticks (100g)
Rich tea biscuits (200g)
Rich tea finger biscuits (250g)
Tesco Value rich tea biscuits (300g)

DAIRY

Almond milk
Cheese
Cottage Cheese
Cream
Cream cheese
Evaporated milk
Rice milk
Sour cream

SOUPS

All cream-based soups
Pureed vegetable
Tinned black bean
Tinned green pea
Tinned split pea

BISCUITS

Digestive biscuits (400g)
Digestive biscuits (500g)
Organic digestives (250g)
Reduced fat digestives (400g)
Tesco Value Digestive biscuits (400g)

DAIRY

Cheese (low-fat)
Cream cheese (light)
Crème fraiche (low-fat)
Frozen yoghurt (low-fat, low-sugar)
Ice-cream (low-fat)
Sour cream (light)

SOUPS

Tinned chicken noodle
Tinned lentil
Tinned tomato

READY MEALS (CONT)

Tesco Finest chicken korma & peshwari rice (chilled, 550g)
Tesco Finest Chilli beef noodles (chilled, 450g)
Tesco Finest Lasagne (chilled, 600g)
Tesco Finest Tandoori chicken masala & rice (chilled, 550g)
Tomato & mozzarella bake (chilled, 340g)
Vegetarian lasagne (chilled, 430g)

YOGHURTS AND DESSERTS

**Apricot summer fruits yoghurt
(Healthy Living light 4x125g)**
Apricot yoghurt (low-fat 150g)
**Blackcurrant red fruit fromage frais
(Healthy Living 4x100g)**
Black cherry yoghurt (low-fat 150g)
Black cherry yoghurt (Tesco Finest 150g)
Black cherry yoghurt (Tesco Finest 450g)
Champagne rhubarb yoghurt
(Tesco Finest 150g)
Devonshire fudge yoghurt
(Tesco Finest 150g)
**Guava & passionfruit light yoghurt –
tropical pk (4x125g)**
Hazelnut yoghurt (low-fat 150g)
Honey-topped greek style yoghurt (140g)
**Mandarin & orange yellow fruits fromage
frais (Healthy Living 4x100g)**
**Mango & papaya yellow fruits fromage
frais (Healthy Living 4x100g)**
Mango light yoghurt – tropical pk (4x125g)
**Morello cherry red fruit yoghurt
(Healthy Living light 4x125g)**
Natural yoghurt (low-fat 200g)
Natural yoghurt (low-fat 450g)
Natural yoghurt (low-fat 1kg)
Orange blossom honey yoghurt
(Tesco Finest 150g)
**Peach & apricot yellow fruits fromage frais
(Healthy Living 4x100g)**
Peach & apricot yoghurt
(Healthy Living light 200g)
**Peach & apricot light yoghurt – tropical pk
(4x125g)**

**Peach & vanilla summer fruits yoghurt
(Healthy Living light 4x125g)**
Peach crème fraîche dessert
(Tesco Finest 2x170g)
**Pineapple & passionfruit yellow fruits
fromage frais (Healthy Living 4x100g)**
**Pineapple light yoghurt – tropical pk
(4x125g)**
Prune yoghurt (probiotic 170g)
**Raspberry & black cherry red fruit yoghurt
(Healthy Living light 4x125g)**
**Raspberry & cranberry red fruit yoghurt
(Healthy Living light 4x125g)**
Raspberry crème fraîche dessert
(Tesco Finest 2x170g)
**Raspberry red fruit fromage frais
(Healthy Living 4x100g)**
**Raspberry summer fruits yoghurt
(Healthy Living light 4x125g)**
Raspberry yoghurt (Healthy Living light 200g)
Raspberry yoghurt (low-fat 150g)
Raspberry yoghurt (probiotic 170g)
**Red cherry red fruit fromage frais
(Healthy Living 4x100g)**
Scottish raspberry yoghurt
(Tesco Finest 150g)
Scottish raspberry yoghurt
(Tesco Finest 450g)
Strawberry and cream yoghurt
(Tesco Finest 150g)
Strawberry and cream yoghurt
(Tesco Finest 450g)
**Strawberry red fruit fromage frais
(Healthy Living 4x100g)**

YOGHURTS AND DESSERTS

Black Cherry yoghurt
(Tesco Healthy Living 200g)
Bourbon Vanilla yoghurt
(Tesco Finest 150g)
Lemon Curd yoghurt
(Tesco Finest 150g)
Strawberry yoghurt
(low fat 150g)
Peach Melba yoghurt
(Tesco Value low fat 125g)
Value yoghurt low fat (4x125g)

MILK AND PROBIOTICS

Cranberry (probiotic drink)
Pink grapefruit
(probiotic drink, 4x100g)
Pink grapefruit
(probiotic drink, 8x100g)

YOGHURTS AND DESSERTS (CONT)

**Strawberry red fruit yoghurt
(Healthy Living light 4x125g)**
**Strawberry summer fruits yoghurt
(Healthy Living light 4x125g)**
Strawberry yoghurt (Healthy Living light 200g)
Strawberry yoghurt (probiotic 170g)
Swiss black cherry yoghurt
(Tesco Finest 150g)
Swiss black cherry yoghurt
(Tesco Finest 450g)
Toffee yoghurt (Healthy Living light 150g)
Toffee yoghurt (low-fat 150g)
Valencia orange yoghurt
(Tesco Finest 150g)
Vanilla yoghurt (Healthy Living light 200g)
White peach yoghurt (Tesco Finest 150g)

MILK AND PROBIOTICS

British pasteurised semi-skimmed milk
(Dairycrest 568ml/1pt)
British pasteurised semi-skimmed milk
(Dairycrest 1 litre)
British pasteurised semi-skimmed milk
(Dairycrest 1.136 litre/2pt)
British pasteurised semi-skimmed milk
(Dairycrest 2 litre)
British pasteurised semi-skimmed milk
(Dairycrest 2.272 litre/4pt)
British pasteurised semi-skimmed milk
(Dairycrest 3 litre)
British pasteurised semi-skimmed milk
(Dairycrest 3.408 litre/6pt)
**British pasteurised skimmed milk
(Dairycrest 568ml/1pt)**

couscous

Coriander & lemon couscous
(110g pack)
Couscous (1kg pack)
Couscous (500g pack)
Mediterranean couscous
(110g pack)
Wild mushroom couscous
(110g pack)

**British pasteurised skimmed milk
(Dairycrest 1 litre)**
**British pasteurised skimmed milk
(Dairycrest 1.136 litre/2pt)**
**British pasteurised skimmed milk
(Dairycrest 2.272 litre/4pt)**
British pasteurised standardised
homogenised milk
(Dairycrest 568ml/1pt)
British pasteurised standardised
homogenised milk
(Dairycrest 1.136 litre/2pt)
British pasteurised standardised
homogenised milk
(Dairycrest 2.272litre/4pt)
British pasteurised standardised
homogenised milk
(Dairycrest 3.408 litre/6pt)
Fresh organic pasteurised whole milk
(arla 568ml/1pt)
Fresh organic pasteurised whole milk
(arla 1.136 litre/2pt)
Fresh organic pasteurised whole milk
(arla 2.272 litre/4pt)
Organic pasteurised semi-skimmed milk
(arla 568ml/1pt)
Organic pasteurised semi-skimmed milk
(arla 1.136 litre/2pt)
Organic pasteurised semi-skimmed milk
(arla 2.272 litre/4pt)
Organic pasteurised semi-skimmed milk
(arla 3.408 litre/6pt)
Orange probiotic drink (4x100g)
Orange probiotic drink (8x100g)
Original probiotic drink (8x100g)

FATS/OILS/DRESSINGS †

Butter
Coconut Oil
Hard Margarine
Lard
Palm Oil
Peanut Butter
Salad Dressings (regular)
Tropical Oils
Vegetable Shortening

FATS/OILS/DRESSINGS †

Corn oil
Mayonnaise (light)
100% Peanut butter*
Peanut oil
Salad dressings (fat-free/low-sugar)
Sesame Oil
Sunflower oil
Vegetable oils
Vinaigrette

OTHER DAIRY

Buttermilk
Cheese (fat-free)
Cottage Cheese (low-fat or fat-free)
Ice-cream (low-fat and no added sugar)
Sour cream (fat-free)
Soy cheese/low fat
Soya milk (plain/low-fat)

FATS/OILS/DRESSINGS †

Canola oil/rapeseed oil
Flax seed oil
Mayonnaise (low-fat/sugar)
Olive Oil
Salad Dressings (low fat/sugar)
Soft margarine (non-hydrogenated, light)
Vegetable Oil Sprays

SNACKS

Cereal/Granola bars
Chips
Chocolates
Crisps/Pretzels/Tortilla chips
Ice cream (regular)
Jelly
Popcorn (regular)
Rice cakes
Sorbet

CONDIMENTS/SEASONINGS †

Ketchup
Mayonnaise
Tartar Sauce

SWEETS

Jelly babies (250g)

SNACKS

Dark chocolate (70% cocoa)
Popcorn (light, microwaveable)

SNACKS

Food bars (20–30g carbs, 12–15g protein, 4–5g fat)

CONDIMENTS/SEASONINGS †

Chilli Powder
Extracts (Vanilla etc.)
Flavoured vinegars/sauces
Garlic
Herbs/Spices
Horseradish
Hummus
Lemon/lime juice
Mustard
Peppers (all-types)
Salsa (low-sugar)
Soy sauce (low-sodium)
Teriyaki sauce
Worcestershire sauce

SUGAR AND SWEETENERS

Corn syrup
Glucose
Honey
Molasses
Sugar (all types)
Treacle

BEVERAGES

Active glucose drink (380ml)
Active orange drink (1 litre)
Active sparkling orange drink (all)
Active sport drink (lemon and orange)
Alcoholic drinks (In Phase II a glass of wine and the occasional beer may be included)
Fruit drinks
Kick cola stimulation drink (250ml)
Kick stimulation drink (all)
Prune juice
Regular coffee
Regular soft drinks
Sweetened juice
Watermelon juice

SUGAR AND SWEETENERS

Fructose

BEVERAGES

Diet soft drinks (caffeinated)
Red wine (In Phase II)
Unsweetened fruit juices

SUGAR AND SWEETENERS

Aspartame
Hermesetas Gold
Splenda
Stevia

BEVERAGES

Bottled water
Decaffeinated coffee
Diet soft drinks (no caffeine)
Herbal teas
Instant hot chocolate (light)
Soya milk (low fat, plain)
Tea (with skimmed milk)
Tonic water

FRUIT JUICES

Pure Apple juice (3x200ml)
Pure Apple juice (6x200ml)
Pure Apple juice (1l)
Pure Apple juice (4x1l)
Pure Apple juice (6x1l)
Pure Apple juice (1.5l)
Pure Orange juice smooth (3x200ml)
Pure Orange juice smooth (6x200ml)
Pure Orange juice smooth (1l)
Pure Orange juice smooth (4x1l)
Pure Orange juice smooth (6x1l)
Pure Orange juice smooth (1.5l)
Value Apple juice (1l)
Value grapefruit juice (1l)
Value Orange juice (3x200ml)
Value Orange juice (1l)

A personalised Gi diet to suit your lifestyle?

At Tesco eDiets, we can provide you with a tailored Gi diet to suit the way you live your life, your health requirements, your food preferences and your weight loss objectives.

Click on **www.TescoDiets.com** and complete our FREE Diet profile. When you join we'll provide you with your first week's personalised meal plan and shopping list. Subscriptions cost just £2.99 per week*.

The Tesco Gi Diet is only available at Tesco eDiets, the UK & Ireland's leading online diet destination.

*minimum 10 week initial subscription

What we offer...
Did you know eDiets world-wide has helped more than 1,250,000 people achieve a healthy lifestyle since 1997? Not surprising when we offer all of this:

1) Customised weekly meal plans & shopping lists
2) Personalised fitness plans & workouts
3) Confidential access to nutritional experts
4) Peer group support & encouragement, 24/7
5) A host of tools & tips to help you succeed
6) And now you can earn Clubcard points too!

The largest range of low and medium Gi products in the UK now at Tesco

Formerly President of the Health & Stroke Foundation of Ontario for fifteen years, **Rick Gallop** is the author of the international bestseller *The Gi Diet*, *Living the Gi Diet* and *The Gi Diet Pocket Guide to Shopping & Eating Out*. He lives in Toronto.

The archetypal accidental author, **Hamish Renton** holds a first degree from Cambridge, an MBA and a number of other professional qualifications. He works for Tesco and has special responsibility for Diet and Health. He lives in Hertfordshire.

The authors would like to thank their families – Ruth and Kate, Poppy and Reuben – for putting up with them during the writing of this book. Thanks also to the Tesco laboratories at Oxford Brookes, Reading and Melbourne Universities for doing a first-class job and to Barb and Sam, Theresa, Patricia, Carolyn, Nicki and especially Angela for helping to steer the project to its successful conclusion.

The Montignac Boutique and Café Since 1994
The original low Gi destination

160 Old Brompton Road
London SW5 OBA
Tel/Fax +44 (020) 7370 2010
www.montignac.co.uk
(See our website for mail-order)
mail@montignac.co.uk

Opening hours:
Monday - Fridays 8.30am-9.00pm
Saturday 8.30am-6.00pm
Sunday 10.00am-5.00pm

Special catering enquiries welcome
(Two days prior notice required - thankyou)

Also available from Rick Gallop and Virgin Books:

RRP £10.99 / ISBN 0 7535 0918 0

RRP £9.99 / ISBN 0 7535 0882 6

The original international bestseller – now fully revised and updated.

All the extra advice and support you need to stay motivated, along with 100 delicious recipes and new food lists so you can create your own meals.

RRP £4.99 / ISBN 0 7535 1032 4

A pocket-sized reminder on which foods to buy at the supermarket, what to look for on labels and how to stay on track when eating out.

'Excellent advice for weight loss, based on healthy eating guidelines.'
The Times